LANGUAGE AN

Dorothy S. Stric
Celia Genishi and Donn

ADVISORY BOARD: *Richard Allington, Kathryn Au, Bernice Cullinan, Colette Daiute,*
Anne Haas Dyson, Carole Edelsky, Mary Juzwik, Susan Lytle, Django Paris, Timothy Shanahan

MW01073879

continued

For volumes in the NCRLL Collection (edited by JoBeth Allen and Donna E. Alvermann) and the Practitioners Bookshelf Series
(edited by Celia Genishi and Donna E. Alvermann), as well as other titles in this series, please visit www.tcpress.com.

Language and Literacy Series, *continued*

Engaging Writers with Multigenre Research Projects

A Teacher's Guide

Nancy Mack

Foreword by
Ken Lindblom

TEACHERS COLLEGE PRESS

TEACHERS COLLEGE | COLUMBIA UNIVERSITY

NEW YORK AND LONDON

Published by Teachers College Press, 1234 Amsterdam Avenue, New York, NY 10027

Library of Congress Cataloging-in-Publication Data

Mack, Nancy.
    Engaging writers with multigenre research projects : a teacher's guide / Nancy Mack.
      pages cm. — (Language and literacy series)
    Includes bibliographical references and index.
    ISBN 978-0-8077-5685-0 (pbk. : alk. paper) — ISBN 978-0-8077-5686-7 (hardcover : alk. paper) — ISBN 978-0-8077-7404-5 (ebook)
    1. English language—Rhetoric—Study and teaching (Higher) 2. Report writing—Study and teaching (Higher) 3. Academic writing—Study and teaching (Higher) 4. Interdisciplinary approach in education. I. Title.
    PE1404.M33 2015
    808'.0420711—dc23   2015013585

ISBN 978-0-8077-5685-0 (paperback)
ISBN 978-0-8077-5686-7 (hardcover)
ISBN 978-0-8077-7404-5 (ebook)

Printed on acid-free paper
Manufactured in the United States of America

22 21 20 19 18 17 16 15   8 7 6 5 4 3 2 1

Contents

Foreword

There's a reason why Nancy Mack was the first person I invited to write an "EJ in Focus" (an in-depth introductory essay) when I became editor of *English Journal* (2008–2013). Nancy is one of the finest teacher-scholars I have ever known. Her advice is based on her many years of classroom teaching experience, on her wide reading across the fields of English education, psychology, rhetoric, working-class studies, linguistics, and more, and her writing is always infused with her keen syntheses and critical insights. What's more, Nancy has a unique way of melding all this into a useful and thoroughly enjoyable read.

So it is no surprise that *Engaging Writers with Multigenre Research Projects: A Teacher's Guide* is an engaging, must-read for teachers of all subjects and levels who care about helping students to develop their voices and deepen their critical reading and writing abilities.

Exploring multigenre research is necessary today. For decades, there was little change in genre. But email and IMs transformed the speed and levels of formality with which we communicate. Then, Facebook statuses and Tweets raised the stakes by making commentary more public and concise. Pinterest and Instagram brought visual communication to a new level, and blogs, Glogster, and infographics allowed us to merge print and visuals for smartphone screens. New genres appear constantly now. It's an exciting time, but it can also be daunting for someone trying to teach people to become more effective communicators. Nancy Mack's work transforms an intimidating array of genre conventions into a powerful storehouse of options that help writers become more dexterous and better able to learn about the new genres they will surely face in the future.

With chapters on conducting interviews, researching nonfiction, narrating events, creating poetry, reporting information, writing academic arguments, using graphics, getting feedback, and writing for real audiences, *Engaging Writers with Multigenre Research Projects* is amazingly comprehensive. The book throughout includes connections with the Common Core State Standards, and a lengthy appendix offers a clear alignment showing how the assignments suggested in *Engaging Writers with Multigenre Research Projects* connect directly with specific anchor standards. Teachers and administrators who feel constrained by standards will appreciate how this crosswalk makes clear how excellent, authentic writing instruction can be completely in synch with CCSS, and they can use Nancy Mack's chart to demonstrate that seamless alignment to potentially skeptical administrators, parents, and others.

But the real gems in this book are the flashes of insight and the witty ways of teaching Nancy has developed. You will see how hamburgers can help students learn to incorporate direct quotes more effectively and encourage students to cite more conscientiously. You will see how imagined cellphone apps can help students add drama and suspense to data-driven nonfiction. You will learn how having students collect the best of their own sentences and reflecting critically on the complex patterns of those sentences will help students increase their repertoires as writers, regardless of whether you require students to learn grammar nomenclature.

Woven throughout the text are brief forays into research to help teachers understand how well-founded Nancy's ideas are in contemporary and long-respected scholarship. Multigenre research projects are fun and creative, while also being rigorous—truly engaging students in very high levels of critical thinking.

The approaches also demonstrate Nancy's profound respect for students and the homes and histories they bring with them to class. A leader in studies of academics and socioeconomic class, Nancy has developed her multigenre projects in ways that allow people to celebrate and closely examine the social and economic contexts within which students live, learn, and grow. Thus, attention to social justice is built into her teaching, and readers will appreciate how the book, particularly the chapter on interviewing, works for all students, even those who are new to the United States and are just developing their skills in English language.

Each chapter begins with a brief discussion of the background and research related to the major concept of the chapter, and then moves quickly into teaching strategies for motivating students to understand and become excited about the work, practical ways of organizing the actual learning, and materials for assessment. Nancy has also developed a companion website that includes all materials mentioned in the text, including the handouts that are beautifully created. Looking through these materials, I am reminded of how generous Nancy is with her experience and ideas. You'll feel like you've found that smart, understanding, and encouraging colleague you've always looked for.

Ken Lindblom

Introduction

Multigenre projects are an effective, flexible way to combine research, analysis, and creativity into a compelling story told through diverse genres. In a multigenre project all the traditional elements of a research paper—quotations from experts, works cited, explanation, synthesis, and analysis—are brought to life as students animate information with emotion and imagination. When I first assigned multigenre research projects, I knew they had great potential for student engagement because the very day I was collecting them, my students were already badgering me about when their projects would be returned. Students did not just want to know their grades; they wanted to share their projects with family and friends outside of the classroom.

The projects that are the focus of this book can be termed *multigenre folklore research*, in that writers supplement and juxtapose archived textual sources with interviews conducted with family and community members who have first-person experiences with the topics being investigated. Writers then communicate the multifaceted knowledge they have acquired through carefully selected genres and graphics. Building the report from real-life genres invites students to use their individual strengths with graphics, media, music, and art and challenges them to master unfamiliar genres. Folklore research topics can be about family, community, or local interest groups and offer writers opportunities to document, represent, and analyze the lives of real people. For instance:

- Amanda Pappert researched her great-grandfather who worked in a Kentucky coal mine and dramatized the safety problems that maimed so many workers and affected their families. Amanda created a scrapbook with a short story, journal entries, newspaper article, allegory, poems, maps, and many family photographs.
- Carmel Morse focused on a mid-20th-century wide-screen Cinerama theater that had existed in her neighborhood and interviewed the projectionist who now shows these movies in his basement. The circular pages of her project are housed in a 16-mm movie canister. Carmel composed her report through letters, flyers, historic photographs, newspaper articles, memoir, poetry, diary entries, and an epitaph.

- Danielle Burrows interviewed a group of air force nurses and created a composite story about a helicopter pilot recovering from being shot down in Iraq. Her project featured a newspaper article, blog, stream of consciousness, short story, photographs, diagrams, and maps, all contained in a binder covered with a military-issue shirt.

Multigenre writing challenges students to experiment and assemble various genres and modalities in order to develop dynamic elements into a coherent presentation. These meaningful projects provide a powerful learning experience about writing, language, ethical representation, and critical thinking.

The use of diverse genres stretches writers to incorporate many voices and points of view in dialogue with one another. For example:

- Heather Topp's project began with the desire to memorialize a relative who lost his life in the Pacific during World War II. Heather was able to read his letters to his sister about his life aboard the USS *St. Lo*. During the process of selecting genres, Heather decided to learn more about Kamikaze pilots who took the lives of more than 100 sailors on the ship. She added a webpage describing a Japanese public monument to Kamikaze pilots and their religious faith.
- In her project, Rachel Dunlap dramatized an incident of racism when a young, dark-skinned Hispanic boy is denied entrance into a diner where his lighter-skinned father awaits. Rachel researched historic texts in order to portray the viewpoints of bystanders as well as the fearful, bigoted owner. She further complicated the events in her play with more genres in which the victimized boy grows up to become a father who forbids his daughter to have Black friends and rationalizes that he must protect his family from being rejected by White people. Her project ended with a eulogy for the father, explaining that he later changed his beliefs and accepted new family members from other races.

These multigenre research projects contain layers of facts, stories, and analysis, incorporating contradictory viewpoints and complex social forces that complicate what might have been previously reported as basic, one-dimensional information (Mack, 2002). My students would testify that the ethical struggle to portray the story of people and places they value is a rich learning experience that required them to learn many new writing skills (Mack, 2006).

HISTORY OF MULTIGENRE WRITING

Multigenre writing can trace its origin to many trends in literature, multimedia, and composition scholarship. Many classic literary works contain multiple perspectives that are enhanced by the use of other genres housed within a larger whole: *A Midsummer Night's Dream*, *Dracula*, *Spoon River Anthology*, *Flowers for Algernon*, and *The Color Purple*. Likewise, many newer young adult novels have captivated readers by telling a story in several different genres: *I Am the Cheese*, *Nothing but the Truth*, *Tears of a Tiger*, *Making Up Megaboy*, *Monster*, and *Give a Boy a Gun*. Some novels even incorporate links to websites: *Click Here (to Find Out How I Survived Seventh Grade)*, *39 Clues*, and *Skeleton Creek*. The use of multimedia has given rise to award-winning documentaries, business and educational slide presentations, and multimodal interactive websites. Scholarship in multimodal writing is advancing our understanding of how students engage with graphics, audio, and video as integral parts of their composing process (Jocson, 2012). Another fertile area of composition scholarship is research into genre theory that has expanded the notion of genre as only a format into exploring how genres can be analyzed as complex social practices (Devitt, 2014). A genre analysis approach better prepares writers for a future that will include new genres that can hardly be imagined today. In the future, writers will certainly experience rapid changes in how texts are composed, formatted, and viewed.

All these connections are important for understanding how multigenre writing found its way into the classroom. During the 1960s, an international conference was held at Dartmouth College to recommend changes in the international English curriculum. In his book about the meeting, John Dixon (1969) reported that teachers need to move away from a skills-based curriculum that was teacher- and product-centered. Dixon cited curriculum scholar James Moffett (1965), who advocated having students write about the same event in several genres. Later, Moffett's (1973) radical redesign of language arts textbooks combined activity cards, games, recordings, and paperbacks, and featured several small booklets devoted to models of different genres that students were to imitate. In the 1970s and 1980s, many teachers were introducing students to writing as a process and encouraging experimentation with early forms of multimedia. At that time, I had middle school students produce skits and plays for reel-to-reel audio and video, and we used photography and photographic slide shows to enhance their writing and research. Many of my assignments asked students to combine graphics with writing in various genres. For example, students composed picture books that contained grammatical sentence structures, restaurant reviews with scaled models, and informative paragraphs on cereal boxes. Teachers at all grade levels were beginning to encourage students to produce multimodal texts to assume an active rather than passive role in the use of media in their lives.

My first exposure to the multigenre research assignment was when I witnessed a presentation by Tom Romano at a conference in 1988. Romano (1995, 2000, 2013) has three wonderful books about multigenre research writing that continue to inspire me and many other teachers. Many educators have adapted Romano's assignment for different grade levels and purposes. Namely, Camille Allen (2001) has a book for elementary teachers, and Suzette Youngs and Diane Barone (2007) focus on middle school students writing biographies. Cheryl Johnson and Jayne Moneysmith (2005) concentrate on teaching argumentation. Robert Davis and Mark Shadle (2007) argue against traditional research papers and suggest creative assignments instead. As a result of the popularity of multigenre writing, several scholars have written theses, dissertations, and books about multigenre writing. For example, theorist Julie Jung's (2005) book promotes multigenre writing as a feminist approach that encourages empathetic listening from the reader.

BENEFITS OF MULTIGENRE FOLKLORE RESEARCH PROJECTS

Three features make multigenre assignments an excellent context for learning about writing, researching, and language:

- A personal connection to a topic
- Research interviews
- Creative publication

First and foremost, writers need to have a personal connection to what they are writing. This type of engagement immerses students in a meaningful academic task that is purposeful and challenging, requiring time and effort to complete. The extensive research on student engagement led by George Kuh (2010) indicates that challenging, creative assignments are an important factor for persistence and retention in college. I have found that the folklore connection to family, community, and local interest groups fosters a deep level of student engagement. I have read amazing projects about topics that I would have predicted to be boring; however, the writers' authentic interest in their topics has triumphed to draw me into learning about whole worlds I would have ignored. I have learned about the corporate success of women through a project about Mary Kay cosmetics from Bernice Money-Pressel and how close the trenches placed World War I soldiers to their enemies from another student. In fact, for both of the previous examples, the writers were not aware of that information before researching their topics. A successful moment of research can be the motivation a writer needs to create a text that will engage readers.

A second feature I strongly advocate including in a multigenre assignment is research interviews so that writers gain information from a primary source. Knowledge from a real person is more immediate, emotional, and tangible for writers. Students can interview an informant as a class or in teams for a group project. In the case where no interviewees are available, students have found other people who shared similar experiences or experts with knowledge related to their topics such as museum curators. Similarly, teacher Jeannine E. Geise permits her students to use published interviews with local historical figures. The responsibility writers feel for their sources increases the drive to represent the experiences of others accurately and ethically.

A third feature of importance is the creative publication of writing projects. As a non-crafty academic, I am an unlikely convert to embracing paper-folding and glue sticks. My friend Joan Smith convinced me of the importance of offering multiple modes for publishing. Students can envision their project as an electronic presentation or a page-turning scrapbook. The medium is less important than the role of images that the writer visualizes while planning the whole project. Images of what the project will become are considered early and influence the choices of genres, words, and graphics throughout the process. Special projects elicit a higher level of care in how the information is presented. The pride students feel when presenting their projects is enormous. Because innovative publishing ideas motivate students to take pride in their projects, students are interested in proofreading and polishing their writing. (See http://www.nancymack.me/ for a longer list of benefits of multigenre folklore research projects.)

My approach to multigenre research writing over several decades of experimentation has been to engage students in inquiry about topics that are meaningful to them in order to improve their abilities to research, compose texts, and examine language features. Little by little, I developed classroom strategies to scaffold students' learning so they learn from their own writing experiences. I have found that drills with isolated sentences are ineffective and that students learn language features best within writing that is meaningful to them. If school assignments respect their family, friends, and communities, then students' self-efficacy for writing will improve. Likewise, connecting research to issues that are important in the lives of students increases students' identities as academics (Mack, 2006).

Multigenre projects have made it possible for me to create many successful teaching strategies, and yet there is always room for something new to be developed. I would be remiss if I did not credit how much I have learned from preservice and inservice teachers and colleagues where I have taught. I began as a middle and high school teacher, was an instructor in three prisons while pursuing a doctorate degree, and have taught undergraduate and graduate university courses in both English and education departments. Several major grants enabled me to team-teach summer graduate courses with elementary, middle, and high school teachers. In addition, I have shared ideas at many state and national conferences as well as district inservices. My biggest joy has come from the fact that students and teachers have exceeded my expectations and have taught me so much through their willingness to share their multigenre projects and give feedback.

OVERVIEW OF THE CHAPTERS

By writing this book, I hope to share more widely what I have learned about the benefits of multigenre research writing with students who are preparing to teach as well as teachers already in classrooms. Readers are encouraged to use the information in the following chapters in whatever way best suits their needs, from individual minilessons to undertaking an entire project, remembering that there are many ways to pursue multigenre writing. To assist you in finding what you need to develop a multigenre project, Chapters 1–9 follow the same basic structure, which is tailored to the project's phases and various genres. Each chapter features an introductory section connecting teaching practices to theory; making connections to educational theories is important in order to understand the reasons behind these best practices and how to foster carefully considered goals. Without theory, teaching practices become misdirected, making it more difficult to be taken seriously by peers and administrators. After the Introduction, each chapter includes the following main sections:

- *Motivators and Inspirations.* These activities help students prepare for the minilessons by introducing concepts and piquing interest. It is not necessary to do every one of these, but please give them a try. And if interest is waning, these activities work to improve motivation.
- *Minilessons.* Each minilesson gives step-by-step instructions for covering essential curricular topics. These have been tested by several teachers and were designed to prevent problems that students often have when learning about research and writing.
- *More Strategies and Activities.* These strategies present ideas for teaching specific topics. Select the ones that fit your students and grade level.
- *Tips and Resources.* Additional resources are provided for topics that tend to come up when assigning multigenre folklore reports.

In Chapter 1, I describe my folklore approach and provide activities for brainstorming topics that highlight family, community, or local interest groups. Techniques are suggested for gathering information from interviews and other community resources. Chapter 2 includes strategies for researching academic sources about social issues as well as how to read and summarize nonfiction sources. In Chapter 3, I share how writers can be taught to analyze a genre for its context, format, content, organization, and language. Suggestions are offered for pacing the work and organizing a large, coherent writing project. Chapter 4 is about narrating a major event as a focus for a whole project. I provide minilessons for several types of prewriting, plotting, and revision. Chapter 5 contains prewriting ideas for poetry, allegory, and other types of literary genres. Revision activities explore figurative language, sentence structure, and word choice. Chapter 6 shares innovative methods teachers can use to clarify how students can select, integrate, respond to, and document academic quotes. Endnotes and works cited pages are also discussed. When it comes to composing genres advocating an argument, Chapter 7 recommends that writers should thoughtfully select the rhetorical strategies that best appeal to their audience and promote understanding. I encourage writers to support their claims with reasons, evidence, and warrants and to revise for tone and confusing pronouns. In Chapter 8, I give advice for publishing creatively with graphics, scrapbooks, and multimedia. Directions for making inexpensive paper-bag scrapbooks and interactive pages are presented. Chapter 9 covers the topics of feedback, reflection, and assessment. Reasons for sharing multigenre projects inside or outside the classroom are endorsed. In conclusion, Chapter 10 extends multigenre writing to other content areas such as literature, sociology, history, and science. Examples are given for various grade levels, standards, and purposes.

While finishing this book, I created a large companion website (http://www.nancymack.me/) where chapter handouts can be downloaded and additional strategies are listed. The tabs across the top of the homepage are organized according to the chapters in the book. This website is referenced throughout the chapters to remind you of the extra materials that are available. There are lots of photos of students' projects that can provide inspiration for fun ways to publish projects. Pin your favorites to Pinterest if you like. Check back frequently for new ideas. Please share your problems and successes through the email on the website, so I can post your ideas to share with other teachers. Everyone can benefit from your experiences with multigenre writing projects.

PLANNING AND ORGANIZING A COMPREHENSIVE PROJECT

A very important question for teachers is how much time to devote to a large project, such as multigenre folklore research. Of course, the decision will vary by grade level and amount of class time. For the first time implementing multigenre projects, I would plan for less than the full grading period with three or more days of catch-up inserted when it is needed. In other classes, multigenre writing may be only 3 weeks added to the coverage of a course topic. A whole course theme or group projects are other ways to organize a unit about multigenre writing.

Multigenre writing can actually save class time by effectively incorporating numerous important curricular standards and goals. If K–12 teachers are devoting a large amount of class time to a project, they want to be sure they are covering several of the required standards. As the chapters in this book demonstrate, many standards can become an integral part of this comprehensive project that provides a more meaningful context for learning difficult skills. Teaching at the college level, I feature multigenre writing as part of a 14-week semester course for English education majors, meeting twice a week for 80 minutes. My students' projects are comprised of a preface essay/letter, table of contents, five genres, transitions, graphics, endnotes, and works cited. The whole unit takes 11 weeks, with an additional 3 weeks of the course devoted to other required topics and assignments (see http://www.nancymack.me/ for my schedule for multigenre research projects).

A key component of organizing a class around multigenre projects is establishing student writing groups. I have found that while working on a large project, writing groups play an important role by providing immediate feedback and helping members solve problems. During class, groups should meet periodically to discuss plans for genres, share drafts for revision, and generate questions about the process. Students may select their own groups of three; however, close friends already know about the people and places in their writing and will not be as helpful as strangers in pointing out places in the writing that are confusing or need improvement. In my class, we keep the same groups during the whole project. I give groups specific tasks to accomplish first; then, they discuss other topics as needed. For each session, group members rotate who shares first. Apologies are banned as a waste of group time. Groups frequently call me over to ask questions and pose problems that I often then address with the whole class. Quick pair-shares are also frequently used before prewriting, after drafting, and after revising.

In my experience, writers need specific daily tasks to keep them organized and feeling positive about their progress. Much of the project work is best done in class where problems and frustrations can be addressed. For example, I have embedded using direct quotes from academic sources into this project because this skill is extremely difficult for students who are attempting to master all the nuances of citation. In class, there is daily checking of interview notes, research sources, drafts, and other requirements.

HOW TO USE THIS BOOK

For future teachers who may have been assigned their first multigenre research report in an education class, this book has many suggestions for finding a topic and getting started. Remember that until you have a meaningful topic to pursue, the writing will not be as purposeful. Chapters are devoted to specific genres with lots of prewriting and revising strategies. Don't overlook Chapter 8 about publishing; look at it early for inspiration, as well as the companion website (http://www.nancymack.me/). Preservice teachers can start thinking about how multigenre research projects would fit into their own curriculum. The individual minilessons in each chapter can help with teaching writing skills, such as revision, citation, and proofreading.

Chapter 10 provides examples of how teachers have adapted multigenre writing for different grade levels and goals. All of these ideas have been tried in many classrooms, so you can start with strategies that other teachers have found helpful. Many student teachers have shared their multigenre lesson plans with their cooperating teachers and have found these lessons clear enough to implement as one of their first teaching experiences.

Teachers who pick up this book may already be interested in multigenre writing and have specific needs for their classroom contexts. Think about your own comfort level for making changes. Are you ready to launch into an innovative new project, or do you have specific problems with a particular topic that you need to teach? Leaf through the book and see what might be useful before you tackle it from front to back.

Preservice and inservice teachers should consult the Appendix for the chart showing correlations between the Common Core State Standards (CCSS) and specific minilessons and activities in this book. This correlation chart shows how to cover the required curricular items with innovative multigenre writing projects that marshal the creative energies of students while teaching high-priority skills necessary for success in college. Thus, teachers can promote electronic genres such as slide shows and webpages, as well as more elaborate genres such as grant proposals and technical reports in order to meet the needs of advanced students. Numerous minilessons bring new life to the CCSS with engaging activities by employing highlighters, sticky notes, and other manipulatives to teach prewriting, drafting, revising, and proofreading. (See Chapter 10 for further discussion of the correlation of the CCSS and multigenre projects.)

Content-area teachers, such as social studies and science teachers, are likely to be attracted to this new approach to teaching research papers. For example, the methods in this book for teaching citation have been adopted by first-year college writing teachers as well as writing-across-the-curriculum programs (Preston, 2015).

The range of writing tasks, genres, and audiences can be as wide or as narrow as a teacher needs it to be. Make what you plan to do your own, but be sure to spend lots of time on prewriting. Coming up with the assignment is only the beginning; this book will help you pace the work, keep writers on track, and ensure that specific concepts and standards are scaffolded for success.

CHAPTER 1

Selecting Folklore Topics and Interviewing

When I began assigning multigenre folklore projects, I was amazed at the response from students. I marveled at the poignant stories students shared about their families, friends, and neighborhoods—most of which I would never have known or appreciated without these projects. Too often, there is a disconnect between school and home cultures that prevents students from developing a positive academic identity. In *Ways with Words*, Shirley Bryce Heath (1983) documented the ways that literacy practices at home differed among three economically and racially diverse communities in the same geographic area, causing some children to be less successful in school. However, students whose home cultures are different from the culture of school do have many important literacy skills to share (Moll, 2014). The main difference is that those skills reflect the students' home dialect or language. Part of the disconnect between home and school cultures stems from the belief that some home cultures are deficient and therefore they are positioned as being in opposition to school. Linguistic scholars John Ogbu and Herbert Simons (1998) point to the alienation that happens when the culture and language practices of marginalized groups are devalued in school. Thus, the language arts classroom must be a place where home culture, life experiences, and language practices of at-risk students are validated. Although this validation is significant for the success of all students, cultural affirmation is crucial for students who are struggling because of cultural marginalization.

At the poor, inner-city schools I attended in my Midwestern hometown, we were told in many ways that we were not "cultured." Culture became the orchestra that we were bussed to see and the names of famous artists and the quotes from Shakespeare that we had to memorize. At the time, I felt ashamed and became convinced that my family and friends were culturally deficient. Fortunately, in college I embraced a wider view of culture as something belonging to everyone—with society giving some cultures a higher status than others. In graduate school, I even studied folklore as an ethnographic research methodology and became more interested in observing and learning about the cultural subgroups affiliated by location, employment, interests, and circumstances. When I taught in prisons, I learned about the code of ethics that included "how to do the time and not let the time do you," when theft was justified by someone else's stupidity, and how men with so little would donate to charities. From my husband's rhythm and blues band, I have learned about trading off riffs, lengths of sets and breaks, and the methods bars use to avoid paying a decent wage. Differences in habits and behaviors make cultural groups worthy of study and representation. Tolerance comes from a respectful understanding of our own culture as well as those of others who are our neighbors.

When given the freedom to write about any topic that is meaningful to them, students do not always take the bait. Instead, students often select hackneyed topics such as drug testing, same-sex marriage, gun control, and abortion. Students' families and communities are too often held separate from school and are overlooked as sources of information worthy of investigation and analysis. Students need to be convinced that the people and places familiar to them possess knowledge that is worth sharing. My students are often surprised by the stories they discover during their project interviews. The diversity of topics is impressive (see http://www.nancymack. me/ for a sampling of student project topics). If their lives are kept at arm's length from the classroom, students will always feel some level of discomfort and distrust with their school experiences. Multigenre folklore projects offer a significant way to embrace the cultures of students while also supporting their literacy development.

This chapter provides introductory activities for learning about folklore and brainstorming multiple topics. Viewing a range of attractive projects and analyzing one multigenre project in depth can inspire writers. I share strategies for maximizing the information gained from interviews. Community resources such as local museums and public history can be useful for gathering information.

MOTIVATORS AND INSPIRATIONS

Taking a Culture Quiz

When introducing students to the concept of a multigenre folklore research project, I find it useful to have them take a folklore quiz, in which they identify items as folk culture, elite culture, or popular culture (Simons, 1990). Some items fit into more than one category—for example, a popular video-game about medieval legends that requires expensive online membership. (See http://www.nancymack.me/ for an example of a folklore quiz.) The students are surprised by the array of folklore traditions: baby shower games, high-five gestures, *Canterbury Tales*, emoticons such as ☺, hide and seek, circular barns, knock-knock jokes, and warnings about muggers putting a 20-dollar bill on car windshields.

Learning About Folklore

A common misconception is that folklore is only about fairytales, vampires, or weird events. To correct this false impression, folklore can be understood by breaking the word in half and defining each half. *Folk* refers to common people and their traditions and customs. Of interest are beliefs, customs, pastimes, or foods that are shared by families, neighborhoods, employees, hobbyists, ethnic descendants, and so forth. *Lore* refers to the stories and information shared from person to person. These stories and explanations should be written down, preserved, and analyzed, and are therefore relevant to the language arts curriculum. It is not only the stories and customs of the most elite people that should be studied and preserved. The knowledge that common people possess can be useful to others, such as what it was like living in the past or how an older person coped with a life crisis.

Finding Folklore in Daily Life with a Game

Having students play a folklore bingo game can demonstrate the many types of folklore they already know. On a folklore bingo card, three categories are placed across the top horizontally: family, work, and community. Listed vertically are the categories of stories, artifacts, and behaviors. (See http://www.nancymack.me/ for a folklore bingo card.) To win, players write in examples to fill up a row. Sharing examples in small groups and as a class reveals to the students their many connections to folklore. These categories also make great short writing assignments.

Viewing Folklore Projects

To help writers start thinking about potential topics for a project and visualizing how their research could be presented, I show photographs of student projects with a wide range of subject-matter and publication types. I present two of each type of topic—family, community, and local interest group—as well as examples of scrapbook and electronic publishing (see Figures 1.1, 1.2, and 1.3; see also http://www.nancymack.me/ for more photographs of projects).

MINILESSONS ABOUT PREWRITING

Generating Potential Topics

Extensive brainstorming is the best way for writers to find topics. Writers need to feel a strong, personal connection to their topics, so all the time devoted to finding the best topic is well spent. The wider the scope of possible

Figure 1.1. Family Multigenre Folklore Project About a World War II Sailor by Heather Topp

Figure 1.2. Community Multigenre Folklore Project About a Cinerama Theater by Carmel Morse

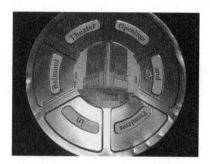

Figure 1.3. Local Interest Group Multigenre Folklore Project About Nurses Serving in Iraq by Danielle Burrows

topics, the more likely it is that all writers will become engaged with the assignment. Brainstorming on just a blank piece of paper results in far fewer potential topics than when writers are given a sheet with sentence prompts. (See http://www.nancymack.me/ for folklore brainstorming sheets.) The prompts are grouped into three major categories: family, community, and local interest groups. Writers should be encouraged to list ideas for all of the prompts even if they are convinced early on that one topic will be the best. To circumvent later problems, writers need to explore more than one idea. Having a plan B is important in case, for example, an informant who is critical to pursuing a chosen topic is unavailable or unwilling to be interviewed.

For the family category, stories can be about current or deceased relatives. After gathering family folklore stories, the Smithsonian Institution created the following categories for its collection (Zeitlin, Kotkin, Baker, & Festival of American Folklife, 1982), which can be made into useful prompts:

Heroes	Rogues	Mischief makers
Survivors	Innocents	Migrations
Lost fortunes	Courtships	Family feuds
Supernatural events	Other stories	Family customs

For the community category, topic prompts can include the following:

Local history	Weather extremes	Land formations/resources
Celebrations	Fairs and festivals	Special events
Founders	Famous residents	Roads
Buildings	Hangouts	Legends and tall tales
School traditions	Changes	Businesses

Because local interest groups is the category least chosen, I suggest spending more time explaining that writers may have a friend, neighbor, or acquaintance with an unusual job, hobby, or past experience. Prompts for local groups can be related to the following:

Sports	Competitions	Music
Drama	Gardening	Skills
Volunteering	Careers	Health concerns
Collections	Sales parties	Flea markets

After listing ideas on paper, writers should share two or more topics with a partner, and then the whole class can discuss initial ideas. Seeing the positive reactions of listeners helps writers to believe that others would be interested in reading about their topic. Writers should also ask family, friends, and acquaintances for ideas because the topics that are closest to us are often overlooked.

For instance, a sibling who is autistic or a relative who has worked in a factory for 20 years are good topics for research and analysis.

Submitting a Proposal

Prewriting is a process through which ideas develop, change, and narrow. For this reason, having writers develop a proposal can foster an ongoing dialogue about the potential stories and events that may become the focus for a project. I ask writers to provide a favorite and a backup topic, including why each topic is meaningful and whom to interview as well as when and where the interview will take place. For their favorite topic, writers should list related subjects that can be researched in academic journals and books, especially all the social issues that might be connected to their topic. Three to five issues should be chosen, such as gender, race, social class, sexuality, and physical ability. (See Chapter 2 for a longer list of social issues.)

I respond to the written proposals and often suggest that writers look for one event to serve as a centerpiece for their project. I also point to potential problems: events that are too far in the past to find interviewees, people who are too busy to be interviewed, topics that are too large such as a person's whole life, and stories that are too emotional such as the death of a relative. If the story is too personal to be shared with other members of the class and the teacher, then a writer should select another topic.

MORE STRATEGIES AND ACTIVITIES

Analyzing a Model Text

A good way to introduce multigenre folklore research projects is to have students read a model project orally and analyze it. This project should be of a high quality that is achievable and inspirational to writers. To emphasize the diverse voices and genres within the model, I assign different readers for each genre and character within a play, as well as a different person to read the endnotes as they occur. Students then reflect and discuss the following: reasons for one genre being the most powerful and effective, suggestions for another genre piece that could have been added, ways that a multigenre report differs from a traditional research paper, and evidence that the author did a good job of researching the topic. (See http://www.nancymack.me/ for a model multigenre text, as well as a list of websites with multigenre projects from several grade levels.)

Conducting Effective Interviews

Setting clear goals for the interview process helps writers find rich ideas for stories to preserve. As part of the research for my assigned multigenre project, I require a minimum of three separate interviews with two different informants in order to gain diverse perspectives. The first interview with the main informant should take place as soon as possible and should be more exploratory, whereas the second interview is often conducted after drafting has begun and specific details are needed. An early deadline for the first interview is important so that writers have time to revise or totally change topics, if necessary. It is not uncommon for a third of the class to modify or change their topics as a result of finding unexpected information during the first interview.

In some cases, the writer may need to find another person to interview to supplement the first interview. For example, one student had interviewed her father about his military experiences in the war. Her father gave factual information but was not forthcoming about his reactions to combat; he was happy to be interviewed but was just not a talkative person. Through a local veterans' organization, the student was able to interview other members of the military who served at the same time and were willing to share many small details about their experiences.

For each interview, I require two accompanying documents: raw notes taken during the interview and a one-page response journal, explaining what was gleaned that was interesting, useful, or problematic, as well as what information was expected or surprising. For the best results, journal entries should be written no more than 24 hours after the interview. I permit audio recordings, but they are not a substitute for written notes. Email and phone interviews are also permitted but generally require more follow-up than face-to-face interviews.

Interviewers need to consider how to explain the assignment to the interviewee, make the interviewee comfortable, and respect the interviewee's rights. (See http://www.nancymack.me/ for an interview release form that can be used if projects will be publicly published.) Developing a list of 10–20 potential questions in advance helps the interviewer feel more confident. However, interviewers must also be astute enough to follow up on responses and even explore a whole new topic that may arise. To help students analyze which types of questions will be most effective at eliciting stories, I have the class conduct a practice interview with myself or an invited guest. I assign groups the following different roles: asking questions, taking notes about each question and response, timing the length of the response, judging the effectiveness of the responses, and writing follow-up questions. Then, the class analyzes the most and least effective questions. Interviewees tend to respond well to questions that ask them to elaborate on events that they rank as best or surprising. Open-ended questions that connect to emotions such as loyalty, fear, or humor usually garner strong responses. (For additional interviewing strategies, see Figure 1.4; see http://www.nancymack.me/ for information on interviewing assisted living residents and exploring urban legends.)

Figure 1.4. Interviewing Strategies

Specific strategies can help in coping with or avoiding problems during interviews, as follows:

- Nodding and giving verbal praise encourage the interviewee to give more details.
- To promote empathy and give time to think of a follow-up question, repeat what was said, using the language of the informant.
- Maintaining eye contact or an overly long pause can encourage a quiet interviewee to speak.
- To avoid bias, ask the interviewee about misconceptions of outsiders or other generations.
- A rambling interviewee can be interrupted by asking about something physical such as a button on a shirt or an object in the room.
- Asking to see photographs or artifacts can help the interviewee remember small details.
- Calling attention to sensory details such as smells, sounds, and colors can stimulate forgotten memories.
- Interviewees who were part of a group can recall how the group determined membership, managed behavior, and distributed power.
- To encourage a quiet person to elaborate, include another family member or colleague who knows about the event or circumstances.
- To give the interviewee power, ask if there are additional questions that should have been asked.

TIPS AND RESOURCES

Visiting Local Museums and Historic Sites

Writers can count on docents and museum staffs being very knowledge-able about their collections. Behind-the-scenes information about display preparation and artifact acquisition gives writers interesting details to report. For example, an interview with the retiring custodian for the Annie Oakley Museum provided one student with new perspectives about visitors and changes to the displays. An archivist from the Rock and Roll Hall of Fame Museum told another interviewer that guitars belonging to famous musicians are given their own seat on a plane when they are flown in for donation. A local historian, librarian, or journalist can be a font of information. Sometimes, a town library or local university will have noncirculating historic books, documents, recordings, and artifacts. Writers are excited to discover stories and information that the general public may not know.

Documenting Public History

Public history emphasizes the experiences of average people rather than only famous individuals. Writers can collect the perceptions of several people about one historic event or across generations about the same social issue. This type of project works well for a whole class to explore. Judith Steider had her high school students collect information about conduct and dress codes in their school district. Students organized themselves by decade and found informants to interview. In the school board office, they even found a document from the late 1800s that defined *public display of affection* as holding hands, punishable by suspension from school.

Selecting interesting topics for their multigenre projects ensures that writers are motivated and off to a good start. Students need to discover that the people from their community have valuable cultural knowledge that makes excellent content for writing. Students can immediately begin interviewing people to search for stories worthy of preservation. Chapter 3 will enhance the information gained through interviews by guiding students in how to find academic texts with information related to their topics.

CHAPTER 2

Researching and Reading Nonfiction Sources

Everyone needs to know how to research information, whether that information is about how to improve a health problem, where to get a good price on a computer, how to repair a window, or whether a new movie is worth seeing. Research not only provides answers to questions and solutions to problems; finding information can be satisfying and even amazing. For example, my students have found that abandoned subway tunnels exist in Ohio, feathers were collected from hunters during World War II to insulate winter coats for soldiers, and a police report exists for a murder that took place in an insane asylum during the late 1800s.

For multigenre research projects, writers need all kinds of information, from brief facts to lengthy research studies based on analytic theories. Students are often astonished that academic scholarship can be found that directly relates to the social issues implicated in their projects. One student told me, "I ended up reading a whole book about research on male bonding for my project about our tradition of going to football games with my dad and brother." Another student, who wrote about a devastating tornado, located research about how people respond to losing all their possessions. Rather than being depressed, this psychological study found that people focus on being grateful for having survived a disaster and often resolve to rebuild and start over. This information gave the writer new insight into how her neighbors and family coped with a traumatic experience.

Writers of folklore projects must decide how to describe the real-life experiences of people who are important to them—not just whether to portray an event as positive or negative, but how to render the many conflicting factors involved. Portraying the experiences of others ethically is a big responsibility, especially so as not to stereotype or devalue someone's life. Researching facts improves accuracy, and researching social issues through published academic scholarship enriches analysis and interpretation.

The Common Core State Standards emphasize several types of research and research writing. The editor for a national college composition journal, Richard Larson (1982), critiqued the assumption that there is one clear research paper format that should be taught to all students. In fact, my colleague Richard Bullock had graduate students interview professors in several different academic departments and found that not one common paper format was assigned. To imply that there is one type of academic research misrepresents the many ways that academics seek and report information. Consequently, focusing on research strategies for finding and reporting information are more useful goals than simply teaching one generic format. Academic writing requires many more skills than one format or genre can teach.

This chapter provides strategies for determining which type of academic research to seek and how to use keywords and search engines to find sources. In preparation for citation of academic scholarship, which is discussed in Chapter 6, minilessons are offered for writing summaries and selecting quotes from experts. In addition, strategies are suggested for creating factual infographics and checking the reliability of websites.

MOTIVATORS AND INSPIRATIONS

Reading a Model Multigenre Text

Writers can be introduced to the type of research that could be incorporated into their projects by reading aloud a student example of a genre that cites academic research about social issues and focusing on the use of quotes. I have the class highlight all the direct quotes in the example and discuss the choices that writers make when incorporating different types of information. (See http://www.nancymack.me/ for an advice column example.)

Listing Targeted Information

I ask each writer to generate a list of factual information that their audience will want to know or will make their writing more realistic in the areas of history, geography, daily life, economics, dates, weather, news, statistics, fashions, fads, terminology, slang, and so forth. The students then divide the list into facts to be researched during interviews and facts to be gained from textual sources. My students have enjoyed researching slang, dialect, and technical language used in particular time periods, locations, and careers.

Selecting Social Issues

I suggest guiding the class to brainstorm a list of social issues that relate to folklore topics, such as the following:

Gender	Race	Social class
Sexuality	Physical ability	Body type
Ethnic heritage	Age	Location
Ethics	Identity	Power
Status	Mental health	Learning style
Relationship bonding	Codependence	Abuse
Personality type	Education	Religion
Values	Birth order	Communication styles
Leisure activities	Economics	Nationality
Immigration	Politics	Income

Then I ask writers to select four social issues that are related to their individual topics. In pairs, they share their social issues and make a list of specific issues to research.

MINILESSONS ABOUT RESEARCH

Looking for Analytic Academic Sources

I encourage writers to find more than simple, factual sources with general information and to research academic sources, which are more analytic than popular books, magazines, and websites. A credible academic source usually fulfills the following criteria:

- The author is associated with a college or university.
- The text is printed or hosted by a scholarly journal, university press, or academic publishing company.
- The text is peer reviewed by other scholars. (This is usually documented on the journal or publisher's webpage.)
- Other scholars cite the text. (This is a linked number located beneath the entry in the search engine listing.)

Some search engines like Academic Search Premier, JSTOR, and Google Scholar screen out commercial websites. By going into the advanced settings, a search can be limited to articles, specific fields such as social sciences, and dates. When students show their sources to me, I check which ones are academic prior to their reading them for information and quotes.

Using the right key words to find sources is essential. For folklore topics, students almost always begin by searching for topics that are too specific. For example, searching "Xenia tornado" or just "tornado" is too specific; searching "disaster resettlement" or "disaster recovery" gained better results. More or newer sources are found by clicking on the "cited by" link under the title. In addition, many search engines also provide bibliographic entries in MLA, APA, and other formats that can be copied and pasted into a bibliography to save time.

To find additional useful sources, writers should take a close look at the works cited or references page of one of their best sources. I often read the works cited prior to reading an article, in order to hunt for other sources. After the class completes a summary activity, which is described in the next section, I read the titles from the works cited and have students give a thumbs-up or thumbs-down as to whether I could find more information for the topic that I am researching. This also demonstrates to students why writers should create a works cited page—for the read-more-about-it effect. As they find good sources, students share with the class what they have found and the methods they employed. By using interlibrary loan and requesting books from the university repository storage, my students have located amazing documents from the early 1900s. This type of academic detective work can be very exciting.

Finding Key Words for Writing Summaries

Having students write a summary for a source can improve comprehension and assist in preparing for writing. The following activity also helps writers find key words for doing searches. My colleague Joan Smith introduced me to a Word Tournament activity that involves the whole class in debating and voting for which words are most representative. First, students are given a brief nonfiction article (one to two pages) about a high-interest topic. Readers highlight the most representative key words as the article is read aloud. Pausing after each paragraph gives writers time to choose words. Next, a large tournament bracket is drawn or projected on the board that starts with eight slots on the left and ends with one on the right. The class quickly nominates eight words. To solicit more discussion, words appearing in the title cannot be nominated. Words are placed randomly in the slots on the left. Then, for each of the four pairs of words, students debate which word is more representative for the article. Students give reasons why a word is more useful for a reader searching for information about that topic. We take a vote and record the winner in the slot to the right. The same procedure is followed for the winners in each bracket, until the class determines the single most important word for the whole article.

To practice writing a summary, students select five to six words from the board and the title of the article used for the tournament activity. For highly technical or specific words from the article, the class can generate a list of synonyms. Students write one word each on small sticky notes. Similar ideas are grouped together and then rearranged in order of significance. Students then compose a one-to-three sentence summary using key words and any necessary filler words. This process helps students get away from the original phrasing in the article. Summaries should be brief. My students have problems understanding that a reference to the author and/or the title of the article should be incorporated into a summary for readers to be able to search for the article; therefore, I provide a list of potential sentence stems. (See Figure 2.1 for examples of sentence stems.) Present-tense verbs are used in writing the summary: *explains, reports, notes, suggests, hypothesizes, states, claims,* and so forth.

Figure 2.1. Summary Sentence Stems

Examples of summary sentence stems that can help writers get started:
- [Author], a [subject] scholar, **explains** that . . .
- In ["Title"] [author] **reports** that [subject] . . .
- The article ["Title"] **notes** that [subject] . . .
- In an article about [subject] [author] **explains** that . . .
- [Subject] has been studied by [author] who **suggests** that . . .

In my class we share several summaries for the article and discuss the similarities and differences. Students practice this skill again in small groups or pairs. I have found that before I ask students to write a summary of a longer academic article, the class needs to discuss why and where authors use key words. Key words help the text to be clear and well organized. Authors often repeat key words by placing them in titles, subheadings, opening and closing paragraphs, and first sentences of body paragraphs. Each student then composes a summary for the same article with key words selected from the previously noted places. This activity also can be used to stress the importance of skimming prior to reading a difficult text.

MORE STRATEGIES AND ACTIVITIES

Selecting Quotes

During the first reading of an article, a writer may think everything a scholar says seems important, but quoting too extensively from sources weakens a piece of writing. I recommend that writers only include a quote if it is significant, brief, and well written. A quote may be selected because it

- reveals an important fact or unique definition,
- explains a thoughtful reason or overlooked social factor,
- expresses a strong opinion, or
- is a witty summary or eloquent point.

Moreover, as drafting begins, writers may discover that a different type of quote is needed, so I recommend that my students mark several potential quotes as they are reading a text. Then it is easy to return to the source and find a specific passage. Although different nonfiction genres use different types of quotes of different lengths, the most effective quoted passages are generally only one to three sentences long. Quoting whole paragraphs is used more for literary analysis or philosophical critiques and even then is used sparingly. When writing college papers, it is always best to analyze the citation practices for that discipline. As might be expected, biologists, economists, and historians quote and cite sources very differently (Hyland, 2004). Students should be reminded that the goal for incorporating a quote into writing is not to be a substitute for the writer's own words but should be provocative enough that the writer can respond to the quote and elaborate upon it. The spotlight should remain on the writer and not the author of the quote.

Creating Informative Graphic Genres

Because a multigenre research project emphasizes the differences among genres, writers should consider whether a graphic genre would be a useful way to display basic information. Factual information is best displayed in a visual format; otherwise, the facts become too repetitive or simplistic to be reported as a news or magazine article. Folklore projects might contain a timeline, family tree, map, or chart, templates for which are available in word processing programs and online websites. Groups can each be given a different infographic to evaluate for the ease of reading information and report to the class. Pinterest is a good source for examples. My students enjoy crafting a turning information wheel to display factual information (see Figure 2.2 for an example and http://www.nancymack.me/ for a pattern and directions for making a fact wheel). They have used the fact wheel to display information about PTSD, prices of food during the Great Depression, and statistics about immigration.

TIPS AND RESOURCES

Reading Websites Critically

Some people will believe anything they see on the Internet, on TV, or in print. A webpage about saving the endangered Pacific Northwest tree octopus can be shared to demonstrate how gullible people can be. Regretfully, unreliable information isn't usually this obvious. A general Google, Yahoo, or Bing search can pull up webpages that cite no author, are out of date, or are biased. The following are websites that can be unreliable because of how

Figure 2.2. Fact Wheel from Janie Freund's Multigenre Project About an Air Disaster in Germany

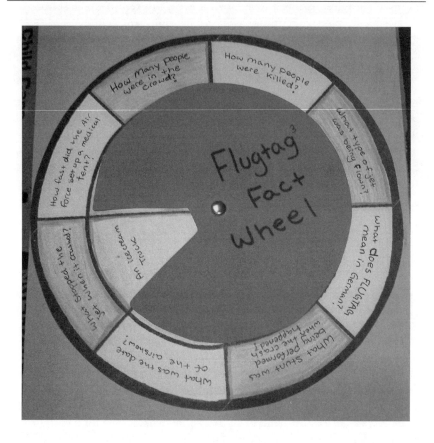

they are created: blogs, tweets, wikis, forums, personal websites, political or religious websites, editorials, Wikipedia, and most .com websites. I remind my students that reading critically is being smart enough not to believe everything they read. This is different from criticizing, critiquing, or just being plain negative. Reading critically involves careful analysis and evaluation. To do this, readers must read a text several times, asking questions of the text and looking closely at what the author chose to include in the text and what was ignored or left out. Earlier in this chapter, I provided criteria for evaluating the author and the source of the publication. In addition, the texts, whether digital or print, should be evaluated for credibility. (See http://www.nancymack.me/ for a list of suggestions for evaluating a text for credibility.) As an in-class activity, peers can check the credibility of one another's sources.

Asking for Help

If researchers are frustrated or are spending hours trying to find sources, the strategies they are using are not effective. I remind students that librarians are the experts. Most libraries take phone calls or even provide instant messaging to respond to questions. In addition to books and journals, libraries have video and audio sources, noncirculating historic documents, and other archives. Some museums also have libraries and archived resources. Another source might be a professor who wrote an article or book who would respond to an email inquiry about an area of interest. One student emailed a professor who had studied NASCAR racing, and the professor provided access to recent academic papers delivered at a national popular culture conference.

Challenging students to find academic information for their multigenre projects teaches the research skills necessary for all types of college writing. Reading analytic sources about social issues helps students use scholarly writing to interpret life experiences. While students are interviewing and searching for sources, Chapter 3 explains how writers can begin sizing up the genres that they might use in their projects. The next chapter also provides important suggestions for keeping a large project organized.

Studying Genres and Keeping Organized

Most professionals have to write reports, proposals, or presentations that are crucial for their career advancement. These high-stakes writing assignments have very specific requirements. My experience with this type of writing is that each business or institution requires something a little different. Moreover, technology advances so quickly that new platforms for composing appear frequently and become essential to most careers. Everything changes; even the conventions for social media writing change. Adapting to change may be more important than mastering one limited type of writing, or genre. Understanding how to read, analyze, reproduce, and adapt a genre will prepare students to present themselves and their ideas confidently.

Modes of writing are different from genres. *Mode* is the term for the larger rhetorical strategies that writers use such as narration, description, definition, comparison, information, argumentation, and persuasion. Regretfully, traditional teaching tends to focus only on general modes rather than specific genres. These terms can be confusing to students. Moreover, composition scholar Robert Connors (1981) argued that assigning writing by modes has been largely ineffective because most real writing employs several modes within one text. For example, a testimony before Congress can involve information, definition, narration, argumentation, and persuasion.

Genres name a specific type of writing that authors actually compose such as blogs, letters to the editor, memoir, and magazine articles. Creating assignments in terms of genres is more familiar and realistic to students. Much of the research into genres has been focused on how writers compose and adapt genres in particular workplace contexts (Bawarshi & Reiff, 2010). Consequently, each workplace genre is different, just as each teacher's assignments are different. Because genres are more than a format, many genre scholars such as Amy Devitt (2014) advocate that genre analysis should be taught. Analyzing a new genre involves a close reading of an example text for the traits of context, format, content, organization, and language. Because the Common Core State Standards specify teaching older genres such as historic documents, students can use genre analysis to understand genres that are less familiar to them. In addition, students need to know how to modify the genres they write in order to suit a particular purpose. Writers must tweak a genre to emphasize a different feature or aspect of the content. Thus, a sports journalist might introduce a story about a particular player differently, depending whether the emphasis is on a controversial issue, a personal backstory, or some unique perspective about the sport. Good writing is less about following rigid rules and more about understanding the current conventions in order to adapt them creatively for a specific intent.

This chapter emphasizes strategies that are useful for a lifetime. Activities help writers analyze both familiar and unfamiliar genres. A list of genres is provided to help in selecting which genres will be utilized in the folklore projects. Strategies are included for planning the order of genres and transitions between genres. Tips are shared for effective drafting and maintaining the progress of the whole project.

MOTIVATORS AND INSPIRATIONS

Seeing All Texts as Genres

To begin thinking about genres, students can be asked to examine a common object that has writing on the surface. My colleague Gerry Nelms has used a soft drink can for this activity with his students. The class can determine several genre traits that occur on all soft drink cans, such as name, contents, calories, and so forth. The class can also list brands that innovate upon the original genre pattern by incorporating new or unusual features.

Analyzing Changes in Genres

A familiar example of genre change is a novel remade as a movie. Students in small groups can be asked to analyze major changes that were made when a specific novel was produced in the new genre of film. In addition, they can propose changes that would be required if a favorite novel were to be developed into a genre such as a videogame or television series. For example, *Fahrenheit 451* might make an interesting videogame in which books had to be saved from being burned. The class can also consider which changes are necessitated when a short story or a play is translated into a movie.

Examining Historic Genres

A more difficult task for genre analysis, which is emphasized in the Common Core State Standards, is to examine an older genre and determine its traits. Student groups can be asked to analyze historic documents such as the Declaration of Independence, the Constitution, the Bill of Rights, or Lincoln's Second Inaugural Address to determine the social context, organization, and linguistic features such as word choice, style, and sentence structure. The students can then parody the historical genre for current times—for example, preparing a Students' Bill of Rights or a Worker's Declaration of Independence.

MINILESSONS ABOUT GENRES

Discovering Genre Traits

Part of the fun in authoring a multigenre project is becoming acquainted with a wide range of genres, some of which may be new to writers. Therefore, writers will need to become familiar with a number of genres in order to make good choices about which genres to include in their projects.

In this activity, I provide student groups with an extensive list of genres arranged alphabetically (see Figure 3.1, List of Genres for Multigenre Projects, and http://www.nancymack.me/ for an even longer list).

The first step is for different groups to organize the list by one of the following categories: familiarity, similarity, mode (narrative, informative, or argumentative), length, and person (first or third). The reorganized lists are shared with the class to draw attention to genre traits.

To conduct a whole-class modeling of genre analysis, the class examines one model document in small groups. I like to use vacation brochures because they are readily available. The class creates a list for each of the designated genre traits (see Figure 3.2)

Reporting About Genres

New genres may seem difficult until they are broken down into traits and smaller features. In the following exercise, the class is polled to find out which genres students are most likely to use in their projects. Then, each group chooses a different genre from the list to analyze and teach to the class, or individuals may wish to select an unusual genre to present. Information about a genre can be researched in several ways: real examples, how-to books and websites, and interviews with people who frequently write in that genre.

Genre presentations should consist of a model, list of traits, suggestions for writing, and active practice. Reports can be posted to a class blog instead

Figure 3.1. List of Genres for Multigenre Projects

Adventure Magazine Story	Fashion or Parent Magazine Article
Memoir	Scene from a Play with Cast
Allegory or Parable	and Set Descriptions
Myth, Tall Tale, or Fairytale	First Responder or Police Report
Annotated Map	Scrapbook Pictures, Captions,
Newspaper Editorial or Advice Column	and Memories
Award Nomination or	Future Goals or Bucket List
Acceptance Speech	Sermon or Prayer or Church Bulletin
Newspaper or Magazine Feature Story	Ghost Story
Birth Certificate and Announcement	Short Story
Newspaper or Magazine	Glossary or Dictionary Entries
Human Interest Story	Stream of Consciousness
Business Letter or Corporate Memo	Graduation Certificate and Speech
Obituary, Eulogy, or Tribute	Tabloid Article or Gossip Column
Campaign Speech or Nomination	Grant or Project Proposal
Organizational or Business Newsletter	Talk Show Interview or Panel
Classified or Personal Advertisement	How-To or Directions Booklet
Personal Letter	Teacher or Counselor Report
Comedy Routine or Parody	"I Am from" or Two-Voice Poem
Poem in Free Verse, Rhyme,	Textbook Chapter or Media Slides
or Rhythmic Rap	Infographic or Information Wheel
Comic Strip or Graphic Novel Chapter	Travel Guide with Historic Locations
Picture Book	Informational Brochure or Infomercial
Informational Program	Vacation Brochure with Descriptions
Postcards from a Trip or Vacation	Journal, Diary, or Blog Entries
Dramatic Monologue	Wanted Poster or Bulletin
Product Descriptions and Reviews	Legal Brief or Testimony
Emails, Texts, or Tweets	Website
Public Service Announcement	Letter of Apology or Complaint
Eyewitness Statement or Testimony	Wedding License and Vows
Resume or Job Application	Letter of Recommendation
Facebook or Social Media Posts	Wikipedia or Encyclopedia Entry
Reunion Newsletter or Holiday Letter	Letter to the Editor
Family Tree or Timeline of Events	Yearbook or School Newsletter
Scene from a Movie with Camera Shots	Lyrics for a Song or Ballad

Figure 3.2. Genre Analysis Traits

- Social Context of the genre: Note the role that the author takes, intended audience, cultural group, location or place, historical time period, conventions and traditions, purposes and motives, status or power, relation to other genres, likely responses or reactions, significance of the results, and possible future actions or outcomes.
- Format of the genre: Note the medium (paper, electronic, oral); layout or arrangement; length; and the number and type of headings, sections, paragraphs, sentences, graphics, lists, charts, diagrams, font, and colors.
- Content included in the genre: Note the type of information, objectivity, generalities, specific details, reasons, logic, metaphors, emotions, examples, facts, opinions, statistics, research findings, historical, dates, places, names, anecdotes, quotes, sources, and addresses.
- Organization utilized in the genre: Note the type of opening, thesis, order and relationship among sections, transitions, conclusion, appendix, epigraph, and endnotes.
- Language used in the genre: Note the type of sentences, tone, style, vocabulary, word choices (technical terms, dialect, slang, jargon, acronyms), use of first or third person, punctuation, and capitalization.

of being done as a demonstration, if time is limited. Active participation helps students engage with the genre traits. Here are some fun possibilities that can be done as a class or in groups:

- Colormark the traits in an example genre.
- Record examples of the traits onto a graphic organizer that lists the categories.
- Compose an example genre for a humorous topic that demonstrates the traits.
- Explain an adaptation of the genre for a specific multigenre project.
- Create a parody of the genre from a historic time period, demonstrating the traits.

MORE STRATEGIES AND ACTIVITIES

Planning the Order of Genres

Near the end of the project process, I used to give students a planning sheet for mapping out the order of their genres. The sheet has columns to lay out the genres in order, noting the content that will be covered in each one (see http://www.nancymack.me/ for the genre planning graphic organizer). Students reported that they found the graphic organizer helpful but suggested that it should have been given out earlier. They told me that they changed their genre choices and their order periodically throughout the project process, so they preferred attaching small sticky notes rather than writing on the organizer page. Students also suggested that it was useful to periodically discuss their plans and problems in their writing groups. Other writers can often suggest changes that the author could not envision alone.

Creating Project Unity with Transitional Devices

Reading a multigenre project can be confusing if the genres do not link clearly to one another. Repeating the names of characters, events, places, and time periods can help connect genres. Tom Romano (1995) refers to these as "repetends." Another helpful strategy is to place shorter quotes, texts, or graphics between the genres as transitions that provide a connection. My students have used several types of transitions to unify their multigenre projects: thematic symbols, photographs with captions, cartoons, timelines, mementos or artifacts, historic documents, famous sayings, quotes, song lyrics, facts, short genres like recipes, journal entries, letters, glossary entries, parts of a longer genre, or a combination of these. Transitional devices should be more than decorative; they can function as additional information about the previous genre, an introduction to the next genre, new information, or a reflection about some aspect of the project. One student used parts of a stream of consciousness, or dramatic monologue, written inside of enlarged cartoon-thought balloons. Some students place their transitions on separate pages, while others include them on the side of each page.

TIPS AND RESOURCES

Including a Table of Contents

A table of contents is an essential element to provide clarity for a multigenre project. I ask students to number their genres in the order to be read and to list three things for each: the title, genre, and author. Numbering each genre will help the reader find the item if the genres are loose in a box or links on a webpage. Knowing the genre before reading helps adjust the reader's expectations, especially when a genre has dialect or vernacular language. I also request that writers list their name as the author for each of the genres they have written. This is because some students incorporate real artifacts such as newspaper clippings or poems by favorite authors. Likewise, some genres appear so realistic that I have mistakenly assumed students did not write them. Students always ask if they should list their transitions in the table of contents. There is no hard and fast rule; however, if the transitions are a genre, they should be listed. Otherwise, famous quotes or song lyrics can be credited in the endnotes. The citation of sources for published graphics is changing. Generally, graphics that are attributed by name to an artist or photographer are listed on the works cited page whereas family photographs are not. Students who ask these types of questions are wisely demonstrating that they have learned that the work of others should be credited.

Generating Effective Drafts

Contrary to popular belief, the most productive first draft is probably one that is rough rather than one that is nearly perfect. Believe it or not, writers who set lower standards for their first drafts tend to start more quickly and write more. Professional writers do not crank out a novel the night before it is due. They write frequently, revise multiple times, and do not expect to produce perfect drafts the first time. There are times when authors do crunch for a deadline, but generally productive writers pace themselves. When I ask my students to do prewriting and drafting in class, I use a timer so that I remain silent and students learn to use their time productively. We start with 5 minutes or less and build to 20 minutes or more.

Some published authors destroy their early drafts, while others donate them to a university library. The widow of Dr. Seuss published one of his rough drafts in the back of a wonderful book entitled *Hooray for Diffendoofer Day* (Seuss, Prelutsky, & Smith, 1998). Seeing the messy crossouts of a famous writer can reduce the unrealistic expectations of student writers. Donald Murray (1998), a Pulitzer Prize–winning journalist, called rough drafts "discovery drafts" (p. 8). In drafting a text, writers should go with the flow because writing quickly is better than second-guessing. I remind students, "You really can't tell what will work best until you see it on the page." Writers need to be kind to themselves; they need to give themselves permission to experiment and explore ideas.

Journaling About the Process

Many professionals work on big projects over a long period of time. One strategy that helps them manage output and satisfaction is keeping a process journal. A process journal is used to debrief various stages, identify problems, and consider solutions. Journals should be free-writes that are quickly done, without worrying about errors in spelling or punctuation. I frequently assign process journal entries at the beginning of class, which students later share with their writing groups and/or turn in to me. First writing about and then discussing successes and frustrations with various tasks that are part of the project help writers with problem solving. Students also journal about their current drafts as a way to clarify meaning and prepare questions for writing group time. By focusing on the specific part of the draft that is difficult or ineffective, students can ask peers to offer alternatives. Writers learn about their own composing process by journaling about which strategies were effective for prewriting, revising, conferencing, proofreading, and so on. Knowing about personal writing preferences can prevent procrastination and writer's block.

Recording Daily Points

In my class, students receive daily points for the work they must complete as part of preparing their projects—interviews, process journals, sources, prewriting, drafts, and so forth. Small goals are set for every class period, and each student's progress is checked. Rubber-stamping is a quick, tangible, and inexpensive way to document the points rather than taking the time to record the points in a grade book. This way, sources and prewriting are not taken away from students to be checked outside of class.

To make rubber-stamping even more efficient, each of my students makes a small booklet for keeping track of stamped points all in one place. This booklet is an idea from my colleague Joan Smith and consists of a folded sheet of paper glued between two small suitcase shapes cut from brown paper (see Figure 3.3 and http://www.nancymack.me/ for pattern and directions for making a points suitcase).

Figure 3.3. Points Suitcase Closed and Open

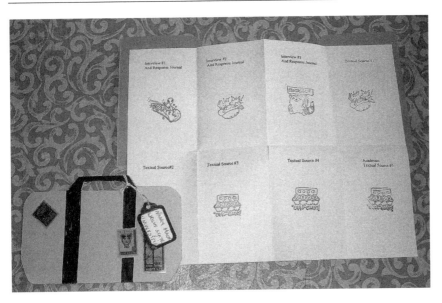

My system works like this. Students open their "suitcase" booklet and place it with the items I am checking on their desks, while they are working on a project task. Students can work ahead, and I can easily tell if someone is falling behind in project preparation. Different stamps can be used each day to encourage meeting deadlines. Process points are totaled when the project is turned in with the stamped suitcase (see Chapter 9). In doing this for more than two decades, I have rarely had a student who has not turned in a completed project on time. Sometimes, writers need to experience how good it feels to keep organized and on track before they will adopt these strategies on their own.

Understanding and analyzing genres is an important part of the curriculum for multigenre research projects. Genre analysis prepares students for careers in the future when they will be expected to produce genres that are unlike the silent and still, black and white texts of today. Writers feel less stressed if they create a flexible plan for the whole project and regularly complete tasks for their projects. Chapter 4 presents prewriting strategies for the narrative story that usually becomes the central genre of the folklore projects.

Narrating a Major Event

Great pleasure, comfort, and wisdom pass from person to person and generation to generation through stories. Preserving the stories of people and places is a considerable responsibility for the present generation and a wonderful gift to future generations. Whether they are writing about overcoming obstacles, accomplishing difficult tasks, or humorous memories, most authors want to represent the events as accurately as possible, all the while keeping their readers on the edge of their seats. Starting is the hardest part. Writers need help getting over the fear of how to begin. I highly recommend prewriting even if writers do not feel ready—even if they are still unsure about their topic. Writing something—even if it is later tossed aside—helps the writer know better which story should be told as well as how it should be told.

Writers should begin telling about a person or a place as an experiment—to get a feel for what will and will not work. In my class after initial topic brainstorming, most students have a person or place in mind for their project, although the focus for the project itself may change. I give points for prewriting activities, even if the genre is never revised or included in the final project. The idea is to get the ball rolling with low-stakes activities such as listing, talking, and free-writing. Students have taught me that one prewriting activity is never enough; it takes multiple prewriting activities to produce a workable draft. Waiting until all the interviewing and research is completed before starting can increase anxiety and procrastination.

I suggest beginning the folklore project by prewriting about the main person or place as a character being portrayed by the writer. Even a group or place has a unique identity that can be thought of as a character. Just exploring the main character will certainly be useful to some part of the whole project. Much like method acting, the writer must do some prep work in order to represent a believable character. The author's job is to give voice to the character, making the story realistic to the reader. Voice is considered a major trait of good writing. Voice, like dialogue, mimics speech, but voice is often more a representation of a complex persona rather than a cardboard stereotype. I think of the narrators whose voices spoke to me as a reader and became believable in *David Copperfield*, *Catcher in the Rye*, *To Kill a Mockingbird*, *The Color Purple*, *Cold Sassy Tree*, *Ellen Foster*, *Speak*, and *Wonder*.

Voice can represent the reactions of a first-person character in a novel or the persona speaking in a memoir. Literary theorist Mikhail Bakhtin (1981) asserts that within each person's words there are many voices of influence from others. The author crafts a complex voice from the influences of many others within the social context, geographic location, and historical time period. Consequently, more than being a report about a series of events, a narrative needs to express the character's point of view or emotional reactions to those experiences. An effective emotional portrayal of voice adds to the reader's feelings of immediacy—of being pulled into the text. Readers appreciate a text that has several emotional layers, with the main character exhibiting conflicting reactions to an event. Close reading of model literary texts, as specified in the Common Core State Standards, helps readers identify strategies that authors use to depict complex characters. After examining model texts, writers can use these same strategies to portray their character's actions, interactions, and inner reactions to events in the narrative.

Dialect is an asset for writing interactions in first person or dialogue. Students can learn to develop their natural ear for dialect through writing narrative genres that portray diverse points of view. Having students use their vernacular language creatively in narrative genres helps to combat the stigma of language differences and affirms home cultures. Not all writing is formal, nor is educated, academic prose effective in all contexts. Thus, language rules become less a matter of good and bad language and more a matter of appropriateness for communicating in a specific context. Students gain experience making language choices for rhetorical purposes rather than merely to avoid criticism from teachers. An inclusive approach to language promotes the success of all students.

The prewriting activities included in this chapter help writers identify a main character's habits, values, emotional responses, and language. Other activities focus on selecting a main event to narrate and mapping a plot line. Revision activities provide opportunities to add action, dialogue, sensory details, and inner thoughts. Several narrative genres are suggested, including memoir, stream of consciousness, dramatic monologue, letter exchanges, and a series of journal entries. Tips are shared for improving word choices, "said tags," embodied dialogue, and the punctuation of inner dialogue.

MOTIVATORS AND INSPIRATIONS

Discovering Narrative Genres in Picture Books

Picture books are a quick way to discover the differences and similarities of narrative genres. Picture books have been written as diaries, letters, stories, biographies, and dramatic monologues. Student groups can each read one book and report on the types of details employed by that genre.

Naming Life Story Genres

A narrative is basically a story that is primarily told in chronological order and can be fiction, nonfiction, or historical fiction. Several genres use the narrative mode to convey a sequence of events. An autobiography is written by a person about his or her whole life, whereas a biography is written by someone else. Both can be too lengthy for this type of project. Memoir is usually shorter than an autobiography and told in first person about events selected by the author as having a particular significance or meaning. Historical fiction is based on events that took place during a specific time period but has some details fictionalized. To help students learn to identify genres, groups can each closely examine examples of two narrative genres and determine the traits that distinguish one genre from another. Groups can help to compile a class list of narrative genre traits. (See Chapter 3 for genre analysis instructions.)

Analyzing a Memoir

For this project, memoir is a useful genre for telling complex life stories because it focuses on events as well as the ways in which the events are meaningful to the narrator (Mack, 2014). I have the class listen to an audio recording of a chapter from a memoir like *A Girl Named Zippy* by Haven Kimmel (2001) or *The Glass Castle* by Jeannette Walls (2005). Then I ask the class to identify the event chosen by the author, the reasons it was chosen, and the meaning the event represents for the author.

Evaluating Narrative Genres

Some genres offer more opportunities for incorporating interesting details than others. An effective way to select a genre for narrating a major event is to create a chart to graph the types of details that can be featured. Four types of interesting details are listed horizontally across the top: action, dialogue, sensory details, and inner thoughts. The genres that are chosen most frequently by students are listed vertically: short story, memoir, play or movie, letters or emails, eulogy, award nomination, journal entries, and stream of consciousness/dramatic monologue. Students then star which details can easily be included in each genre and problem-solve how other details could be incorporated. Carefully selecting a narrative genre can help students avoid the need to abandon a draft and start over later because the chosen genre did not permit enough details.

Considering First- and Third-Person Points of View

For a multigenre project, writers can choose to have some of their genres be in first person and some in third person. Writing in first person gives more opportunities for inner thoughts and emotions. An easy way to tell the difference in point of view is to look at different examples about the same topic, such as an historical event. For this activity, I recommend *The Things They Carried* (O'Brien, 1998), which includes short stories about the Vietnam War. Students can be asked to read sections from several of the short stories and make lists of the traits of both third- and first-person narratives and note the differences. Rarely are stories told in second person.

MINILESSONS ABOUT PREWRITING AND REVISING

Writing in First-Person Point of View

In every multigenre project, several people are represented. The most important people are the main characters, whereas others can be bystanders or more generic community members such as nurses, bus drivers, or waitstaff. One of the assets of this type of project is that the use of multiple genres permits the writer to include contrasting points of view (Mack, 2002). Sometimes, a writer needs to create a character in order to express an oppositional opinion or to demonstrate a different life choice. To help students begin thinking about the characters they will create, I ask them to brainstorm a list of all the potential voices that will be speaking through the genres they are considering for their project. (See http://www.nancymack. me/ for a people, places, and things brainstorming sheet.)

After brainstorming a list of potential voices that will be given power to speak in their projects, writers select one main character and prewrite a list of details related to that person's habits, values, and language style. Writers should imagine this character in action, doing a favorite task, as well as any events that would cause conflict for the character. Jotting down information about what the selected person would say or do in a familiar context helps crystalize details that can stimulate writing. (See http://www.nancymack. me/ for writing in another person's voice expansion sheet.) This activity may be problematic if the writer cannot interview this person or is choosing to personify a place; therefore, writers will have to use their imagination to generate details that will create a believable, complex character. The following prompts can help writers generate details about their main character:

- Identify the character's strongest personality trait.
- Select a fictional character in a book, television series, or movie who best represents that trait.
- List the ways that this character varies from typical cultural stereotypes.
- Invent a scene in which that character is talking with another person and/or is very emotional.

- Imagine hearing the character speaking, the tone of voice, and common greetings or sayings.

Giving voice to a character through writing in first person becomes easier and more effective when writers identify the emotions that will be portrayed. For this reason, I have my students engage in the following activity. As I read a dramatic monologue aloud, students list the many emotions portrayed in the model text. I pause at key places to have listeners jot down a word to represent the character's changing emotional state. After three or more emotions have been listed, students share their lists, drawing attention to twists, conflicts, and surprises. Next, the class discusses how the author used emotion to make the character more complex. I emphasize that writers need to make ethical decisions about which feelings and inner thoughts of their character to represent. The writer must remain true to the values and beliefs of the person being characterized although some emotional responses may be too private or painful to share.

For the next part of the activity, writers first select possible emotions for their character from a long list of many types of emotions. Students can make a timeline of emotional responses for their character, considering how the reactions change or develop from a worried first response to a reasoned decision about what to do.

Finally, students select a genre for a timed free-write from the point of view of a person or place significant to their project. At this stage, the prewriting should be experimental, so the genre does not matter. Students can write a journal entry, letter, stream of consciousness, monologue, or dialogue. Drafts can later be revised to take the form of a different genre. Even a weak free-write can point writers toward a genre or a voice that might work better for their project.

Because writing in first person may not work for every folklore project, students need to decide whether their free-write should be extended into a full draft or not. For quick feedback about the success of the free-write, I ask the class to rank whether their free-write has the potential to be included in their project with a thumbs-up or thumbs-down gesture. Better to experiment early and find that a voice will not work than to waste several days creating a weak draft. However, at the end of the unit, during metacognitive reflection, the majority of my students credit this activity for germinating their central piece. Examining models and prewriting helps writers make early connections to their central character, with structure following next.

Mapping a Plot

Selecting an event as the main focus of a narrative can be difficult if a writer has obtained a long history of a person, group, or place. There will be numerous big and small events to choose from. The good news is that a multigenre project offers several other genres in which different events and time periods can be featured. However, for this activity students must create a main narrative, in which they choose one event to dramatize for readers to vicariously experience. A major life choice such as a military career, surviving the Great Depression, or being a single mother can at first seem not to have one outstanding event for a dramatic focus. In such cases, a composite event can be created that represents the typical frustrations or small acts that demonstrate the personality of the person, group, or place. In class, I ask students to brainstorm factors that can be dramatized: a conflict that involves more than one person, perspectives involved, changes that take place, and multiple responses to the event. (See http://www.nancymack.me/ for a copy of the event brainstorming sheet.)

Ethical problems that may arise are similar to those in writing historic fiction, where some of the details can be documented while others must be elaborated or embellished to dramatize the event. Writers can use endnotes to explain which information was gained from interviews and the ethical decisions related to which details had to be fictionalized because of a lack of information. In most cases, small details such as weather, colors of clothing, and even inner thoughts will need to be embellished. Writers should consult historical books and photographs to gain a sense of what the time period was like. Students can read works of fiction or view movies that contain similar characters or experiences. Small details can be added later, after the basic narrative is drafted. Additional interviews can be scheduled for answering specific questions about an event.

Narrative writing is often hard to organize and control. Writers have problems knowing where to begin. In addition, narratives can turn out to be surprisingly long or short, frustrating the author. For these reasons, students benefit from listing a sequence of smaller actions on a plot graphic organizer (see http://www.nancymack.me/ for the narrative map graphic organizer). I adapted the mountain-shaped graphic used for analyzing the rising and falling action of stories. Students should begin by listing a type of conflict and a specific place for a revealing conversation or action that can be grounded with sensory details. Complications come next that provoke inner worries, fears, and the opinions and warnings of others. Reactions from others and more inner thoughts can close the event and may be linked to other genres that follow.

Some of the common pitfalls of narrative writing include the bed-to-bed narrative that includes mundane details like turning off the alarm clock or brushing teeth; this may be because the brain tends to call up the memory of a specific event by recapping the whole day (Huttenlocher & Prohaska, 1997). In contrast to the bed-to-bed narrative, readers and movie viewers like openings with action or strong dialogue. Also to be avoided is putting all the description in the beginning of the narrative and not including enough description in the other sections. I tell students that a good rule of thumb is to make the climax the longest section of the story with the most descriptive details.

Colormarking a Model Text to Guide Revision

The process of revision can be tedious for teachers and punitive for students. Marking up a student's text is time-consuming for the teacher, and research indicates that the result frustrates and confuses students (Montgomery, 2009). I have found that student-directed revision is more effective when it is specific, concrete, and based on real models, as described below.

I give students an envelope with a graphic of a cellphone on the front. Inside are "apps" printed on small slips of paper. Each "app" describes a revision strategy for one of four types of details that can be added to a narrative—action, dialogue, sensory, and inner thought (see Figures 4.1 and 4.2).

Figure 4.1. Cellphone Envelope and Revision Apps

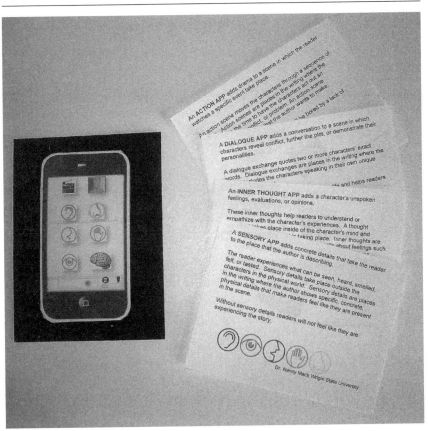

Figure 4.2. Cellphone Apps for Revising a Narrative

An **ACTION APP** adds drama to a scene in which a reader watches a specific event take place. An action scene moves the characters through a sequence of events. Action scenes are places in the writing where the author takes the time to have the characters act out an important event, conflict, or problem. An action scene demonstrates the point that the author wants to make. Without an action scene, readers will be bored by a lack of development and excitement.

A **DIALOGUE APP** adds a conversation to a scene in which characters reveal conflict, further the plot, or demonstrate their personalities. A dialogue exchange quotes two or more characters' exact words. Dialogue exchanges are places in the writing where the author includes the characters speaking in their own unique language or dialect. Dialogue makes the characters come to life and helps readers understand the characters' relationships.

A **SENSORY APP** adds concrete details that take the reader to the place the author is describing. The reader experiences what can be seen, heard, smelled, felt, or tasted. Sensory details take place outside the characters in the physical world. Sensory details are places in the writing where the author shows specific, concrete, physical details that make readers feel like they are present in the scene. Without sensory details, readers will not feel as though they are experiencing the story.

An **INNER THOUGHT APP** adds a character's unspoken feelings, evaluations, or opinions. These inner thoughts help readers understand or empathize with the character's experiences. A thought comment takes place inside the character's mind and intensifies the action that is taking place. Inner thoughts are places in the writing where the author tells about feelings such as worries, guilt, fears, hopes, desires, or exaggerations. Without an inner thought comment, readers will not understand the character's actions or empathize with the character's motives.

First, the class reads a narrative that is either a published memoir or a student model. One of the four apps is explained; then, as a class we colormark examples of that strategy in the model with a colored pencil, after making a color key at the top of the first page. Volunteers share their favorite examples and give reasons why this technique is effective. We examine where and how frequently the author uses this strategy in the whole piece. Next, writers immediately apply the targeted revision app to their draft by writing their new text on a sticky note. Students share some of their revised sections aloud with the class. Then, the second app is read, and the class colormarks examples in the same text with a different color. Examples are discussed and students add that type of revision to their drafts. The activity continues until all four types of revision strategies have been examined and tried. The action and dialogue apps usually need larger, lined sticky notes to accommodate the additional text.

I point out to students that the four revision apps should be used in different places in a narrative text. *Action* or *dialogue* works particularly well as a way to begin a narrative. Jumping into the action or opening with dramatic dialogue will capture readers' attention. Important background information can follow. An opening scene can be a flash-forward followed by a flashback to how things began. Adding dialogue to a narrative is a wonderful way for writers to use the vernacular language that they hear every day. Realistic dialogue can include dialect, slang, jargon, incomplete sentences, interruptions, and silence. Students have a right to use language from their home communities; the National Council of Teachers of English endorsed a statement to this effect in 1974. Including dialogue is the perfect way for writers to show off their home language. *Sensory details* should be spread throughout a narrative. In order for the reader to feel present in the scene, it is particularly important to add sensory details every time the place changes. Research indicates that readers feel what they read because they process sensory writing about smell in the same place in the brain where they process actually smelling something (Paul, 2012). Horror writers like Dean Koontz tend to utilize two sensory details prior to a climactic moment; however, trying to add all five senses may be too much. *Inner thoughts* are less likely to be used by writers and can work well prior to or during action in order to build suspense. Occasionally, a writer discovers through revision of a draft that the genre chosen does not allow for enough sensory details or inner thoughts. Switching genres may be necessary to permit the student to use these important writing strategies. This is why revision should happen during the project process rather than waiting until the very end to revise everything.

MORE STRATEGIES AND ACTIVITIES

Experimenting with Stream of Consciousness or Dramatic Monologue

Stream of consciousness is a relatively modern literary genre that began in the late 19th century as interest grew in psychology. Stream of consciousness is interior thoughts, representing the character's candid, emotional reactions to events within the story. A character's conflicted interior thoughts and feelings are more realistic to readers than a simple description of outward actions. Some authors like James Joyce omit punctuation and capital letters to make the text flow uninterrupted from one thought to the next; however, not all authors omit punctuation. After reading an example of stream of consciousness, students enjoy the challenge of creating a text that reveals the worries and reflections of a person who is central to their project. Similar yet slightly different, a dramatic monologue or soliloquy is another interesting genre in which the character addresses the audience in an effort to explain the reasoning behind his or her actions.

Including Multiple Letters or Journals

An interesting option for the multigenre project is to feature several letters or journal entries that chronicle multiple conflicts, changes, and/or events for the main character. Students have incorporated a letter exchange between two characters that discusses events in two different places such as at war and at home. Others have created multiple journal entries from the main character in order to portray how the character adjusts to a stressful new situation such as emigrating to a new country. Emphasizing inner thoughts and reactions rather than mundane events makes these genres more interesting. In order to clarify the motives for the character's responses, the writer will need to have the narrator retell events and conversations in letters or journals. Students can analyze a multigenre novel like *Monster* (Myers & Myers, 1999) that uses journals or letters to reference previous actions or conversations. Multiple examples of one genre can be spaced throughout the project with other genres placed in between.

TIPS AND RESOURCES

Choosing Words Carefully

A great way to increase awareness of word choice is to highlight or color-mark favorite words in a paragraph or two from a well-written model text. The text is read aloud while students mark their favorite words or phrases. Then, students narrow down their favorites to one or two and write down three reasons that explain why that word or phrase is effective. After discussing their favorite examples from the model text, writers should revise a current draft to add clever word choices. I love this activity because I always learn something new about the model text from the students' explanations. I simply choose a text that I like, but digging deeper to determine how an author crafted the words and phrases to achieve a particular effect takes close reading and analysis on the students' part.

Using "Said Tags" and Embodied Dialogue

"Said tags" are not always necessary, especially if the dialogue is rapid-fire and each speaker is given a new paragraph. The convention for dialogue is that "said tags" are necessary to identify the speaker the first time to avoid confusion and to break up long speeches. Most editors suggest avoiding unusual verbs or even adverbs for tags because they sound artificial rather than like natural conversation. Of course, using the word *said* too often can also be distracting. Writers employ embodied dialogue by adding revealing actions and expression. For example, they might add details about facial expressions, gestures, body position, and/or vocal tone to enrich a scene—unless these techniques are overused. An occasional simile combined with embodiment adds emphasis to a character's dialogue. For example, *She smiled, as if agreeing with everything, and said. . . .* Students can search for examples of this technique in their favorite books.

Punctuating Inner Thoughts

Students often ask about how to punctuate a character's inner thoughts. This interest indicates that a writer is trying something new and is genuinely interested in correct punctuation. Because stream of consciousness is a newer style of writing, punctuation conventions vary. Usually, quotation marks are not used for inner thoughts. Some authors use verbs related to thinking such as "thought" or "wondered." No italics or tags may be necessary if the text is narrated in first person. However, other authors use italics, particularly if the thoughts in question might be confusing to the reader because of the surrounding narration or dialogue. Editor Beth Hill (2012) suggests that inner thoughts should be treated like dialogue and be started as a new paragraph.

Avoiding Tense Shifts

A narrative can be told in either the past or present tense; the writer must decide which tense is preferred and check for consistency. A few sentences of a draft can be rewritten in the opposite tense in order to listen to the differences. When writers are composing dialogue, they may switch from past tense in the narration to present tense in the dialogue. The writer's brain may inadvertently stay in present tense in the narration that follows the dialogue. The only way to catch this type of tense shift is to check for unintentional tense shifts before the final draft.

Prewriting activities help writers construct interesting, complex characters. Mapping out the plot of a narrative event prevents the writing from wandering and writers from becoming frustrated. No matter how wonderful the first draft, specific revision strategies can enhance the types of details that readers appreciate. Chapter 5 introduces several creative genres that students enjoy including in their projects: poetry, fairy tales, allegory, and comics.

Creating Poetry, Allegory, and Other Literary Genres

Reading and writing are reciprocal activities that inform one another. Research indicates that we learn a great deal about writing from reading (Langer & Flihan, 2000). Stephen King, Mark Twain, Benjamin Franklin, Ernest Hemingway, and Billy Collins all report that they learned about writing by examining and imitating the texts of authors that they respected (Wheeler, n.d.). Learning by imitation was a favored teaching method of the Greeks. Educational expert Lev Vygotsky (1978) explains that students can learn skills beyond their ability through the zone of proximal development. In the case of writing, a mentor text provides a zone for apprenticeship through imitation. Learning writing by imitation involves finding a well-written example, closely examining the use of language, and then imitating the style and structure for a new topic. This type of learning fits well with the Common Core State Standards that specify both the close reading of texts and understanding figurative language. Moreover, the close reading of poetry helps students imitate sophisticated language techniques in their writing.

Imitation is one of the most basic ways humans learn. We observe patterns and then imitate them. We find that patterns in music, art, architecture, poetry, and nature are pleasant and even beautiful. Every genre has a textual pattern that can be identified, imitated, and innovated. An innovation upon a genre can become a parody that we enjoy for the similarities to the original genre and the witty changes from the original. Within each genre there are subgenres and even smaller patterns within each unique text. For instance, poetry can have many types of repeating patterns, both simple and complex, such as rhyme, rhythm, and alliteration. Identifying patterns in models of good writing is one way to discover how an author made the writing interesting and meaningful. A scholar of written style, Paul Butler (2002), believes imitation unleashes a beginning writer's creativity; in particular, a model format offers a safe and effective structure that invites writers to insert their own meaning, thus freeing the writer to be original. Imitating the form of a poem can be a challenge, like a puzzle for a writer to solve.

This chapter features learning about poetry through the imitation of patterns. Students use word banks to draft pieces about photographs. Writers can also experiment with unfamiliar genres such as an allegory, two-voice poetry, picture books, and comic books. Activities encourage revision for improvements in figurative language, sentence structure, and word choices.

MOTIVATORS AND INSPIRATIONS

Writing an "I Am From" Poem

A classic poem for students to imitate is "I Am From" by George Ella Lyon (1999). I had the pleasure of meeting Lyon when she did a reading for my class and shared this poem before it was published. The poem references many types of details about individual life experiences. Students enjoy creating poems about themselves first in order to become familiar with the repeating format of each stanza, beginning with the stem line, "I am from." After sharing their poems, students draft an "I Am From" poem for their multigenre project. The poem can chronicle details about the history and values of a person or place represented in their project. Providing a repeating stem line helps students to create a poetic pattern because rhyming poetry can be intimidating. (See http://www.nancymack.me/ for "I Am From" prewriting, expansion, and format sheets.)

Reading Poetry Aloud

Poetry is best read aloud, and a participatory reading can help the class notice repeating language patterns. In this activity, each group is given several copies a poem to perform, emphasizing a repeating pattern of figurative language. Students enjoy silly poems by Jack Prelutsky, Ken Nesbitt, or Bruce Lansky. Each group should receive enough copies of one poem so that they can study and mark their own copies. Groups of four or five make for a raucous reader's theater performance. I usually go over a list of elements that might be repeated in poems. For example, students may notice a repeating pattern of lines beginning with the same word or the use of alliteration or rhyme. (See the section about figurative language later in this chapter for more terms.) After selecting one pattern to emphasize, the whole group decides how they will perform the poem in order to emphasize the pattern. Each group member must read some part of the text aloud and make a gesture or movement. Some parts can be read altogether, or each person can read a different stanza, line, or word. Students can clap, stomp, change levels, or turn around to emphasize words of a similar type. Groups practice their vocal emphasis and movements a few times before performing for the whole class. When each group is done, the class guesses the emphasized pattern and gives examples. The poetry performances help writers become familiar with elements that they then add to their drafts.

Marking Patterns in Model Texts

In this activity, students select a text by a favorite published author, mark any patterns they find in different colors, analyze the patterns, and report on one of their findings to the class. This activity can be done with poetry or can be expanded to include prose. For example, a student examined the poem "We Wear the Mask" by Paul Laurence Dunbar (Dunbar & Braxton, 1993) and explained how the pattern of the first stanza is reversed in the third stanza; instead of beginning with the mask and ending with smiles, the last stanza begins with smiles and ends with the mask. All published writers develop habits and strategies that they use to captivate readers and provoke emotional responses. An endless number of interesting patterns can be found in model texts if readers search for them.

Analyzing a Parody of a Fairytale

Comparing a parody to its referent is an interesting way to map out the pattern of a genre. Fairytales or tall tales work well for this activity because there are many interesting innovations upon the older tales. A storyboard or two-column chart can be used to list the basic plot for both the original version and a newer innovation. Many parodies have a humorous change or twist. For instance, the *Paperbag Princess* (Munsch & Martchenko, 2006) and *Sally Ann Thunder Ann Whirlwind Crockett: A Tall Tale* (Kellogg, 1995) provide critical commentary on gender roles. Once the traditional pattern is identified, students discuss the innovative twist that the modern author used to make the parody serve a different function from the original. Song parodies by Weird Al Yankovic (2014) are also amusing to discuss and analyze. An imitation of a genre becomes a parody when it serves a different purpose. As one component of their multigenre project, students may select a genre to parody by changing the purpose from serious to entertaining or vice versa.

MINILESSONS ABOUT PREWRITING

Brainstorming About a Photograph

One of the most popular prewriting exercises for the folklore project is the photo-write. Students bring one or more photographs to class that directly relate to their topic. The photographs can be of people or places. If a student is using valued family photographs, it is best to make a copy or scan the photographs to be sure that the originals are not lost or damaged. If no personal photographs are available, students can search books or the web for photographs related to their general topic or time period. The Library of Congress website has an extensive collection of historic photographs. Sharing a photo-write poem written by a student from a previous year gives a general idea for the activity. (See http://www.nancymack.me/ for an example photo-write poem.)

Viewing a photograph provokes a writer to include details that would otherwise be difficult to imagine. This point is easy to demonstrate by first asking students to brainstorm details about a topic without a photograph and then doing the same activity while looking at a photograph. Visuals stimulate the imagination. To begin this activity, writers arrange their photographs in front of them, while I give a series of prompts. For each prompt, writers take a few minutes to jot down words that come to mind onto sticky notes. I use the following prompts:

1. List small details that are seen within the photograph.
2. List sensory details that can be imagined in association with this photograph. (Describe the weather or the lighting.)
3. List stereotypical traits that outsiders might wrongly associate with this person or place.
4. List unique personality traits that only you know that are associated with this person or place.
5. Compare a trait of this person or place with an event, animal, object, or element in nature.
6. List something important related to this person or place that should be in the photograph but is missing.
7. List your regrets or sadness about this photograph or a wish that you have for this person or place.
8. List your hopes or happiness about this photograph or pride that you feel about this person or place.
9. Describe what happened before or after the moment this photograph was taken.
10. Quote what the person with the camera might be saying or thinking while taking this photograph.

After brainstorming details and words on sticky notes, writers arrange their sticky notes on top of their desks in the order that they will use for writing. Sticky notes should be discarded if they are not useful, and new ideas can be jotted down. Students are given 10 minutes to quickly draft a poem or memoir about their photographs.

While students are drafting, I spread out paint chips that I have collected from various hardware stores. Each paint company provides descriptive names for various hues of colors. After drafting, students look through the paint chips and jot down words that they might be able to add to their text. Some students look for colors that match something in their writing, while others select words that represent a mood or a descriptive comparison. For example, they might write, "her voice surrounded me like a *misty fog*" or "her hands looked like *weathered barn* siding." Writers add these words to their drafts and share their revisions with the class. Students also enjoy cutting up their photographs and arranging them on paper to combine with their writing. Looking at examples from scrapbook magazines can give writers ideas for balancing sections of text with photos.

Selecting a Character Trait for an Allegory

For their project topics, most students select people or places that they wish to honor with their writing. Consequently, the subject's personality traits are a creative focus for a piece of writing, such as an allegory. For instance, students have written about the positive traits of determination, courage, resourcefulness, and faith. They have also juxtaposed negative traits that caused their person or place conflict, such as fear, aggression, and disrespect for tradition—as in the case of a historic building being neglected or torn down.

An allegory is a story in which the characters are personifications of abstract qualities such as faith, bravery, or greed. Allegories are an unusual genre, so it helps to read and analyze one prior to writing. There are several classic and contemporary examples such as Aesop's Fables, *Young Goodman Brown, Animal Farm, The Alchemist,* and *The Book Thief.* I was inspired to teach this genre when a friend introduced me to *The Book of Qualities* by J. Ruth Gendler (1988), but I prefer to share a student example of an allegory. (See http://www.nancymack.me/ for an example allegory.) In this activity, after reading the allegory aloud, students colormark examples of the traits of an allegory. Then the class examines such features as the use of third-person pronouns, present-tense verbs, and specific details. We discuss the ways that an allegory differs from a memoir or a biography.

Before the students begin writing their allegories, they need to find an abstract noun that expresses a major personality trait that represents or conflicts with their character. I share a list of traits, and students sometimes consult a thesaurus to come up with a trait for prewriting. Next, writers personify the trait as a character and dramatize a life for that character. Writers brainstorm daily life habits, conflicts, and actions large and small that would reveal the traits. After a quick pair-share of potential ideas, writers generate a 10-minute free-write that tells the story of their personified character trait in action. The name of an abstract noun should be substituted for the character's name, and details that are only specific to their real person should be avoided. I suggest that writers jump into the action rather than beginning with their trait waking up in the morning. After writing, students volunteer to share a section of their allegories. Students enjoy the challenge of trying a new genre and often include their allegories in their completed multigenre projects.

MORE STRATEGIES AND ACTIVITIES

Creating Two-Voice Poems

Two-voice poetry portrays two characters' different perspectives about one topic or event. The plot line of two-voice poems works from agreement to disagreement or vice versa. These poems are a creative way to display argumentative writing. A two-voice poem usually has two columns: one for each point of view. If the poet wants the two characters to say something at the same time, the words are placed on the same line in each column. The two characters should have distinctive voices and use different word choices and dialect features. Thus, hearing examples read aloud is helpful because this type of poetry is more effective as a performance.

In the following activity, students first view an example on YouTube and then work in pairs to perform a two-voice poem as a reader's theater for the class. One of the first volumes of two-voice poetry is *Joyful Noise* by Paul Fleischman and Eric Beddows (1988). Students are especially captivated by "A Graduation Poem for Two" (Klose, 1999). Writers begin planning a two-voice poem by each brainstorming diverse points of view for a major event or issue related to their topic. Next, writers work in groups of three to role-play ideas. Two students ad-lib a dialogue, while the third writes down what was said so that the author can decide later whether or not to include the information in a draft of the poem.

Revising for Figurative Language

Both poetry and prose genres benefit from the use of language that is cleverer than its literal use. Metaphors, similes, personification, and other figures of speech delight an audience. However, these literary devices take some time to invent and are seldom generated in a quick first draft. Most students enjoy the emotional effect of these turns of phrase but often do not know their names or how to use them. In fact, figurative language can be found within most popular songs. To prove this point and make students familiar with these terms, I create a brochure with the name of the term, definition, and an example from a song. My examples tend to be from older songs, so I give bonus points for students to supply newer examples. I use the following figures of speech, but there are many more techniques that can be added to this list:

Simile	Metaphor	Extended Metaphor or Conceit
Metonymy	Synecdoche	Personification
Hyperbole	Oxymoron	Alliteration
Assonance	Consonance	Onomatopoeia
Anaphora	Rhythm	Rhyme

After I review two or three terms, students find examples of figurative language in the humorous poems that are later used for the reader's theater activity explained earlier in this chapter. When they are familiar with the terms and examples, writers examine their poetry drafts for opportunities to add figurative language. Writers use small sticky notes to add or change words, and volunteers share some of their revisions with the class.

TIPS AND RESOURCES

Collecting Golden Sentences

A sentence collection is a teaching strategy that I have used for a long time. It helps writers pay more attention to effective sentence structures. The idea is to collect elegant example sentence structures for imitation. I use a yellow highlighter while I am reading papers to mark the single best sentence in each student's paper. When I pass back the papers, I have students write their name and highlighted sentence on a card, which I collect. I organize the file of cards by the topics for minilessons: clauses, participial phrases, infinitives, gerunds, parallelism, similes, semicolons, and so on. I always cite the students' names when I share well-crafted sentences because the praise usually gets passed along to students even if they were in my class a year or two ago.

I like to have students imitate a model sentence during an editing mini-lesson. For writers to be able to imitate the sentence, it is only important to point out the use of a key element, usually a word or an ending to a word. Students can easily imitate a sentence that begins with *if* or ends with an *–ing* element—especially if they first underline the element with a colored pencil or marker. For example, *Expecting nothing worse than a skinned knee, the first responders lounged next to their vehicle* can be imitated by inventing a participial phrase to precede a sentence. If being able to name the grammatical element is important, the name and definition should be presented to the class *after* they imitate the sentence. Naming the elements and defining them prior to imitating them is off-putting. The name is only memorable to writers when it has a personal connection to a sentence they have written and have hopefully taken pride in. After imitation, students can effectively analyze the sentence's structure, meaning, punctuation, and learn the names. Many poems repeat a grammatical element such as in "If I

Were in Charge of the World" (Viorst & Cherry, 1981) (For more examples, see Mack, 2005, 2008, on teaching grammar with poetry.) Students can also join in the search for "golden sentences" by nominating them from their favorite short stories or novels.

Creating Picture Books and Comic Books

Imitating graphic genres is much harder than it seems. There are several helpful books about the conventions used in these genres. For comic books, Scott McCloud (1994, 2000, 2006) explains techniques for developing graphics to tell a story. Writers first familiarize themselves with the techniques of merging words and graphics and then set a reasonable goal for a number of frames or pages. A storyboard can be used to plan the pacing of the plot. Both genres rely heavily on action, so planning how one graphic moves to the next is important. For a multigenre research project, writers should focus on a major event. If drawing is too time-consuming, students can use a website like Pixton that supplies graphics for characters and settings.

Finding and imitating patterns in model texts ensures that writers can stretch to compose difficult or unfamiliar genres. Adding a poem, parody, or graphic story to students' projects can renew interest in their work. Figurative language and complex sentence structures teach important skills and increase the quality of students' writing. Chapter 6 introduces students to the difficult skill of quoting scholars in informative texts that is essential for college writing.

Reporting Information and Writing with Direct Quotes

Most people enjoy sharing new information with their friends. Much of the new content that we learn comes to us through reading textbooks, websites, newspapers, and other information sources. Likewise, most of us write primarily in nonfiction genres on a daily basis when we compose emails, posts, tweets, newsletters, business letters, plans, reports, and presentations. Noted education researcher James Britton labeled school writing that does not communicate information as "dummy-runs," done solely for the teacher, rather than transactional writing that communicates information (Britton, Burgess, Martin, McLeod, & Rosen, 1975). Regretfully, working-class students are required to do much more of this pseudo-writing than more affluent students (Anyon, 1981). An authentic task creates a context in which learning language skills is more meaningful, especially when authors are proud to share information with an audience of friends and family outside of school.

After all the hard work of searching, locating, reading, critiquing, and selecting quotes from authoritative sources, writers need to know the best way to integrate this information into their projects. Requirements for citation should include scholarly articles and books because these are the genres that are the forums for academic writers. The Common Core State Standards emphasize the citation of evidence. However, the larger purpose for citation is joining the academic conversation by engaging in a critical dialogue with others about topics of interest. Responding to academic sources rather than just citing them helps students develop the identity of an academic writer. Linguist Ken Hyland (2002) has studied citation practices in academic writing in many disciplines and reports that "academic writing, like all forms of communication, is an act of identity: it not only conveys disciplinary 'content' but also carries a representation of the writer" (p. 1092). Learning about citation is more than just a matter of accuracy; it is also part of the process of creating a confident identity as an academic writer. Citation practices are connected to differences in how disciplines view knowledge. Hyland (2004) found that instead of the hard sciences' emphasis on facts and statistics, the humanities generally have more citations and direct quotes per paper with more elaboration about the context and author of the quote. Consequently, writers should learn how to integrate, contextualize, and elaborate upon direct quotes, which are more important skills than simply knowing where the punctuation marks should go in the works cited list.

Errors in citation may simply indicate a lack of knowledge about specialized academic conventions, rather than an intention to plagiarize content. I cringe when I realize that most teachers, including myself, spend too much valuable class time stressing the harsh penalties possible for plagiarism infractions. At one university on the first day of class, I was required to have students sign a statement that they had been informed that they could be failed for plagiarism—as if to frighten students into behaving. Plagiarism is a negative experience that no one wishes to encounter, so I can understand why universities would prefer to avoid problems by purchasing a product that promises to do away with plagiarism by screening papers electronically. However, studies confirm that costly plagiarism-detection services are inferior to a simple Internet search (Weber-Wulff, 2014). The national College Composition and Communication Caucus advises that using plagiarism-detection services can have adverse effects on academic integrity by assuming that a student is guilty, creating a climate of mistrust, substituting technology for teaching, and violating a student's privacy. Stanley Fish (2010), a professor of humanities and law, argues that teachers should consider plagiarism less of a moral offense and more of a learning problem. Citation can be presented more positively as learning how to show off evidence rather than negatively as avoiding being caught for plagiarism. Students need an experience in which they gain status from citation—as if they were bragging to their readers about finding really interesting information.

This chapter suggests realistic nonfiction genres that writers can compose to show off the results of their academic research. Innovative methods are presented to analyze and integrate sources by accurately introducing and critically responding to direct quotes. Creating endnotes and works cited pages are also discussed.

MOTIVATORS AND INSPIRATIONS

Reading a Model Nonfiction Text

Writers can read a nonfiction example that contains in-text academic quotes such as an article from the *New York Times* or *Atlantic Monthly* or an advice column. Students can highlight the quotes used in the writing in order to note where and how quotes are used. This is a good way to overview the type of quoted information in a nonfiction genre.

Listing and Analyzing Nonfiction Genres

To help writers select the nonfiction genre that would be most useful for their projects, I ask the class to brainstorm a list of possibilities. The following nonfiction genres are the ones most frequently included in projects by my students:

Advice Column	Grant Proposal	Newsletter Article
Editorial	Counselor Report	Letter of Complaint
Human Interest Article	Social Worker Report	Self-Help Article
Magazine Article	Textbook Entry	Award Nomination

Next I have students select one of the genres from the class list and complete an analysis of that genre's traits, being sure to explain the context, format, content, organization, and language (see Chapter 3 for genre analysis instructions). This task is best done in groups, and then the information is presented to the class. This activity is particularly helpful for students who may not be familiar with genres such as a grant proposal or award nomination.

MINILESSONS ABOUT CITATION

Seeing the Conventions

Writing nonfiction genres necessitates learning many research writing skills—narrowing a topic, searching for authoritative sources, reading those sources critically, and finding cogent quotes to cite (see Chapter 2). This minilesson focuses on the skills needed to introduce, quote, and comment upon a text published by a scholar. What I have seen far too often from writers are what I call "drive-by" citations or chunks of published texts substituted for their own words. Beginning writers often string together a bunch of information from different sources, being somewhat intimidated by the knowledge and sophisticated prose style of published texts. When I was in middle school, I remember doing this type of patch writing—copying chunks of text from various brands of encyclopedias for a report. The sentences were so perfect and the words seemed so smart that I had no way of inserting my own words into the report. Even with quotation marks around copied passages, this type of writing offers no critical analysis. More than just correctly punctuating a quote, writers need to interact with what they have read by integrating it into their writing and commenting upon the ideas within the quote. This is certainly a lofty goal, but one that will serve writers well in gaining a sense of authority in all their academic writing.

The following minilesson features colormarking a model text to focus the eyes and brain on closely examining the text as a writer. Feedback for this activity from students has been extremely positive at all grade levels. Complex text features can be overwhelming to decipher. Colormarking makes the patterns visible so that the text can be analyzed and imitated. The whole minilesson is framed positively as bragging—showing off the knowledge gained through research. Academics do a considerable amount of name-dropping when they write in order to support their assertions and connect their ideas to respected scholars. Likewise, students should be able to present the knowledge they have researched for their projects in a way that gives them status in their writing.

For this minilesson, each class member should have a copy of the same newspaper article or an advice column from a student model multigenre project. (See http://www.nancymack.me/ for an example nonfiction genre with quotes.) Three different colors should be designated for marking the example. A key should be created at the top of the page with one color for each of the following: introduction, quote, and commentary. Colored pencils work best for printed articles with small fonts, while highlighting is bolder and can be used with electronic articles. First, we read the model genre aloud, stopping so students can colormark each part of every citation.

1. Students mark the introduction to the first quote that usually gives the author's full name, area of expertise, and the topic being discussed that relates to the article.
2. Students mark the direct quote itself in a second color, circling the quotation marks surrounding the exact words from the source.
3. Students mark the commentary in the third color. The quote is most often followed by a discussion or commentary in which the writer relates the quote to the particular case being addressed. The commentary is generally longer than or at least equal in length to the quote.

Next, the font for one of the quotes from the model genre should be enlarged electronically to 28 points in order to colormark the punctuation pattern. Students use different colors to mark quotation marks, page numbers, periods, and other punctuation marks, noting which mark comes first. The idea is to force the brain to focus on the little things: dots and dots with tails. The brain prefers to attend to more important things, like the meaning of the whole text (Weaver, 2002). Enlarging and colormarking the punctuation focuses attention on the small marks on the page. I was stunned at how effective enlarging and colormarking the text was the first time I tried it. The result of this strategy was that almost all of my students punctuated quotes correctly in their nonfiction genres—which is remarkable given the difficulty of the task.

Sandwiching a Quote

I use an analogy of a hamburger to present the citation pattern from the previous minilesson before students begin drafting their nonfiction genres. Citation is compared to a sandwich that has an enclosing big bun around a meaty quote (see Figure 6.1). The top bun is the introduction, the meat is the quote, and the bottom bun is the commentary. This visual analogy has been revised many times and is one of my most popular teaching handouts. Recently, I have enlarged the hamburger into a graphic organizer to permit students to write on the graphic in order to practice sandwiching one of their quotes (see Figure 6.2).

Drafting a nonfiction genre is best done during class time when problems can be immediately conquered. By introducing citation practices in a real genre rather than in a lengthy term paper, writers learn how to negotiate authority, elaborate upon the ideas of others, compose scholarly phrasing, and master the nuances of punctuation. I explain the steps for sandwiching a quote in order from top to bottom as students fill out the graphic organizer. (See http://www.nancymack.me/ for copies of both of the hamburger handouts that can be downloaded.)

1. The author's full name is used the first time to introduce the quote. For additional quotes just the last name is used.
2. The author's area of expertise should be mentioned so that the reader knows the information is credible. A brief reference to the author's academic job, such as *sociologist, historian,* or *psychologist,* can be included along with the academic's name. If information about the author is limited, *scholar* or *researcher* can be used, depending on whether the source of information is scholarship or a research report.
3. The major topic that the reader needs to pay attention to in the quote should be included. This should be mentioned with key words in one of the introductory sentences.
4. A formal introductory verb is preferred (see the examples in Figure 6.3), rather than an informal verb indicating that the quote was "lifted," "pasted," "taken," "found," or "copied." (Following MLA style, a present-tense verb is used to indicate how the writer evaluates the information, whereas APA uses a past-tense verb.) Example stem sentences for introducing direct quotes are provided in Figure 6.4.
5. The author's exact words are inserted with quotation marks enclosing the sentence cited from the source. Missing words are indicated with ellipses: three dots with spaces (. . .). Any words inserted by the writer are enclosed in brackets: "She [Eleanor Roosevelt] did not concern herself with the opinions of her critics."

Figure 6.1. Citation Hamburger

CITATION IS LIKE BRAGGING.
Citation makes your work more valued and respected.
A quote can document that you have learned a lot about a topic. Adding commentary makes you look smart.

SANDWICH YOUR QUOTE

INTRODUCTION
• Tell the author's full name.   • Tell the type of expert.   • Tell the topic of the quote.
• Use an academic verb:
points out, explains concludes, notes, comments, suggests, discusses, declares, describes, claims, insists, argues, observes, believes, mentions, remarks, reports, reveals maintains, emphasizes, stresses, expresses, acknowledges, thinks, confirms, implies, states, responds.

QUOTATION
• Give the author's exact words.• Use quotation marks around the exact words.
• Give the page number of the quote in parentheses outside of the quotes: "(7).
• Indicate any changes in wording in brackets: He [Fred].   • Use three dots with spaces to indicate missing words [. . .].

ANALYSIS
• Make your analysis longer than the original quote.
• Try to do one or more of the following:
    ⁄Tell why the quote is significant or interesting.
    ⁄Explain your interpretation of the quote.
    ⁄Extend the author's point to your situation.
    ⁄Give an example or exception to what the expert says.

NO MORE DRIVE-BY CITATIONS

Dr. Nancy Mack
Wright State University

Figure 6.2. Hamburger Graphic Organizer for Practicing Direct Quotes

Quote Sandwich
Author's name
Author area of expertise
Topic of the quote
Academic verb
Quoted words with quotation marks
Page Number
Phrase indicating commentary
Commentary about how the quote fits this case

6. To create the commentary that follows the quote, I ask students to first free-write for 2 minutes about each of three or more of the following prompts:

> ➤ Tell why you selected this quote.
> ➤ Retell the basics of what the author is trying to say.
> ➤ Tell how accurately this quote relates to your person or place by giving an example or an exception.
> ➤ Tell why people should pay attention to and understand this information.
> ➤ Explain the ways that this quote is unrealistic or an oversimplification of the problem.
> ➤ Expand on the expert's point by adding your own ideas.

7. A transitional phrase signals to the reader that the analysis or commentary is beginning (see Figure 6.5). A transitional phrase and the previous free-writes should be used to generate a sentence or more to place after the quote.

Figure 6.3. Verbs for Introducing Direct Quotes

Positive: *advocates, argues, holds, sees, finds, claims, points out, shows, demonstrates, develops, discovers, explores, indicates, proves*

Neutral: *addresses, cites, comments, reports, describes, notes, analyzes, discusses, finds, observes, notices, views*

Tentative: *alludes to, believes, hypothesizes, suggests, proposes, uses, publishes, conceptualizes*

Critical: *attacks, condemns, objects, refutes, suspects, ascribes*

Figure 6.4. Example Stem Sentences for Direct Quotes

The scholar's name [S], area of expertise [E], topic [T], and evaluative verb can all be included in a sentence stem that precedes the quote. Here are some examples of various ways that the introduction could be worded:

[S], a [E] who has studied [T], suggests . . .

[S], who is a [E], condemns [T] in this statement . . .

According to [S], a [E] scholar, research about [T] indicates . . .

A [E] scholar who studies [T], [S], claims . . .

A [E] researcher, [S], has studied [T] and finds that . . .

The effects of [T] have been studied by [S], a [E], who reports that . . .

Addressing the problems of [T], [S], a [E] scholar, explains . . .

Figure 6.5. Example Stem Sentences for a Transition to the Commentary

A transitional phrase is used with the scholar's name [S] and/or the topic [T] of the quote to make a connection to the person or place [P] being discussed. Here are some examples of various ways the transition to the commentary could be worded.

To agree with the quote:

Just as [S] stated, [P] has . . .

As [S] suggests, [P] has . . .

As a result of this [T] problem, [P] has . . .

In [P]'s case, the issue of [T] has . . .

Indeed, [P] has had problems with [T] . . .

To disagree with the quote:

In opposition to what [S] claims, [P] has . . .

Although [S] makes a valid point about [T], [P] has not . . .

Instead, [T] has not been a problem for [P] because . . .

However, [P] is an exception to [S]'s claims about [T] . . .

Unfortunately, [P] has not had the benefit of [T] . . .

Students need to consider which possible nonfiction genres fit with their projects and which can best integrate quotes from academic sources. Students should discuss the reasons for selecting a particular nonfiction genre with a peer. I prefer quality over quantity. Therefore, students should quote scholars only a few times in their project, but they must introduce and respond to the quotes thoughtfully. These citation skills are a critical component for learning about academic writing.

MORE STRATEGIES AND ACTIVITIES

Creating Endnotes

Endnotes are used in academic writing; therefore, students should become familiar with their use for the purposes of both reading and writing scholarship. I find that sharing examples of nonfiction genres and corresponding endnotes from model student projects is helpful for writers to understand how endnotes are used. Endnotes give the reader additional information that would otherwise be a distraction or a tangent. Endnotes can be explanatory, supplemental, or bibliographic. Editors I have worked with prefer endnotes to be used for explanatory information. Think of this as a place to explain decisions made as the author—for example, to describe what information in a genre was changed, altered, or fictionalized. Students often use endnotes to explain their rhetorical reasons for choosing a particular genre. Supplemental information might be defining terms, explaining the historical context, or giving background details. Endnotes can be used for indirect citation of sources; however, the trend in publications in the humanities is to use more in-text citations and fewer endnotes. If a genre would not normally contain a reference to a source, an endnote can be used, which is formatted like the works cited, or the author may want to note that the information came from an interview.

For multigenre projects, I require endnotes to be written in formal language and placed at the end of the whole project, just before the works cited page. The page is titled Endnotes and is double-spaced. The notes are numbered in sequence from the beginning of the project until the end. An Arabic number is placed in the text at the end of the phrase or sentence after the punctuation mark. Putting the numbers into a whole project can be tedious, especially if the writer is unfamiliar with using an automatic insertion tool in a word processing program. Superscript can be done manually and is found within the font choices. Titles may have endnotes for explaining information that applies to the entire genre. Writers who are new to the use of endnotes tend to use too many. Editors are interested in conserving space, so one to two endnotes per genre might be a reasonable number. Footnotes are similar but are used more often in science. They occur at the bottom of the page and are numbered per page rather than throughout the whole document. Most college professors do not require undergraduate students to use endnotes or footnotes. When I share my students' multigenre projects with colleagues, they are impressed that I require endnotes. I like endnotes because they provide a metacognitive analysis of the writer's choices of events, genres, and language.

Punctuating a Works Cited List

Academic disciplines and subfields prefer different citation styles. University professors from different fields would duel to the death over whether MLA or APA should be the preferred citation system. Moreover, major style systems such as APA, MLA, Chicago, Turabian, Bluebook, and Harvard make frequent style changes. So, a quick review prior to creating the works cited list is helpful. I create a puzzle for students to solve. I make copies with a large font size of a correct example works cited list that has articles, books, websites, and interviews. Then I cut apart the entries and the major sections within each of the entries, mix them up, and place them in an envelope. Student groups are each given an envelope and have to reassemble the parts in the correct order. Manipulating the pieces of correct examples is more brain compatible for visual memory than correcting wrong examples (Friedmann, 1983). Some websites will generate bibliographic entries in different formats. I prefer http://www.worldcat.org/ because some commercial websites do not keep up with frequent format updates.

TIPS AND RESOURCES

Finding Answers to Citation Questions

Writers always have questions about difficult citation problems. I have learned to love these questions because they demonstrate a genuine concern about documentation. The most common questions are about citing secondary sources and what to do about multiple authors. I print an example in large font for examination in class. Currently, MLA prefers that the name of the person who originated the quote be used in the sentence and the secondary source where the writer found the quote is noted in parentheses:

> Francis Galton, British scientist and explorer, states that "The American system [of building the railroad] was well-fitted to the needs of the American people; a rough and ready cheap railway entails increased cost for maintenance, but is preferable to a more expensive and finished line" (qtd. in Luckin 448).

I point out to students that the person who said the quote is more important and should therefore come first, and the person who cited it comes last. When citing multiple authors in the text, the abbreviation "et al." is used after the first name:

> Thomas Curtis Clarke et al. state that "The modern railway was created by the Stephensons in 1830, when they built the locomotive 'Rocket'" (1).

For other questions, the Purdue Online Writing Lab is a frequently updated website with information about MLA and APA (see http://owl.english.purdue.edu).

Using Facts in Informative Writing

Within informative genres the placement of facts varies depending upon the genre. Newspapers often present the most crucial facts first, with other related details following. This method is represented by an inverted triangle. Placing the most important information first benefits the editor, who might have to cut something from the article to fit the available space. Other informative genres like a feature article in a magazine or a blog might begin with a hook or interesting details to attract readers, including facts later in the article. Some news magazines present facts in sidebars that are boxed and may include charts, graphs, or pictographs. To construct a realistic genre, students should take some time to examine the conventions of the target publication. (See Chapter 3 for information about how to do a genre analysis.)

Academic writing is an obscure form of writing for students who are less familiar with the genre. Breaking down the integration of direct quotes into smaller tasks makes students aware of the conventions of introducing, quoting, and responding to selected passages. Informative writing is best taught positively through real genres. Likewise, Chapter 7 introduces argumentative writing through reading and writing public genres to forward issues important to students' projects.

Advocating an Argument: Writing with Reasons

The history of argument traces back to the period in ancient history when the Greeks transitioned from a warring monarchy to a diplomatic democracy. To maintain a peaceful democracy, many viewpoints need to be asserted, acknowledged, and affirmed. Public genres are used to draw attention to complex social issues. However, the popular connotation for the word *argument* is misleading. Argumentative writing is not a fight for dominance in which one side declares victory over another. Instead, argumentative writing is a forum for cooperation in which diverse groups advocate for societal improvements. It might seem easier to simplify issues into a disagreement between two sides, but important issues are generally more complicated. For every social issue that affects the lives of many people, there are many sides or perspectives. For example, a disease like alcoholism affects individuals, families, businesses, cities, and nations. Moreover, there are multiple factors that influence those perspectives. Blaming the weakness of one person for alcoholism overlooks the influence of biology, psychology, the economy, geography, society, and many more factors.

Argumentative writing should be about expanding the dialogue. Argumentative writing is emphasized in the Common Core State Standards in order to prepare students for college writing based on academic scholarship. Academics argue by carefully defining the terms, clarifying the facts, establishing criteria, qualifying reasoning, citing credible evidence, and suggesting policy. When real people and places are implicated, argumentative writing must be respectful. I am always impressed that students are concerned about representing people accurately and compassionately in their projects. Writing that matters always involves ethics.

This chapter asks students to examine the reasoning used in real arguments. Writers select social issues that connect to their projects and answer prewriting questions about related facts, definitions, criteria, and policies. Claims need to be supported with reasons, evidence, and warrants. After selecting a genre, writers consider which rhetorical strategies best appeal to their audience and promote understanding. Drafts can be revised for tone and confusing pronouns.

MOTIVATORS AND INSPIRATIONS

Finding Genres with Argumentation

Newspapers are a good source for multiple genres that address controversial issues and present arguments. Student groups can cut out three or more articles, columns, reviews, and/or editorials that address social issues. For each genre, groups identify the social issue, the people directly and indirectly affected, and the economic implications. If newspaper websites are used, groups can post links to each genre and post their analysis lists on a class blog.

Identifying Reasons in Reviews

Reviews are another good source for argumentative writing. Groups can select a favorite movie, album, fashion, television series, book, restaurant, or product and search for reviews. Then each group ranks three or more reviews for the same item. For each review, students identify the number of reasons and rank their quality. Argumentative writing in the form of reviews is helpful for making decisions. Groups can post links to each review and post their ranking lists on a class blog.

Identifying Reasons and Evidence in Proposals

Local government councils deliberate about proposals for changes and improvements. Student groups can search the web for a proposal being considered by a locality, or they can search for a report about a controversial issue under review in many areas, such as wind farms or residential group homes. Groups identify the reasons presented in a proposal and the evidence used to support each reason. Groups can post links to each proposal and post their evidence lists on a class blog. As a challenge, groups can research additional evidence needed to address community concerns or potential problems.

Role-playing Multiple Points of View

The whole class can critically analyze a local controversy reported in the news. After identifying the facts of the case, the class brainstorms a list of the many types of people who are directly and indirectly involved. Then, each of the roles is written on a filing card and given out to class members. On the other side of the card, each student lists concerns or problems that the role might have. For example, a controversy involving an athlete would be viewed differently by a stadium vendor, teammate, coach, recruiter, fan, parent, administrator, religious leader, lawyer, news reporter, and so on. One at a time, students enact the concerns of their role's point of view. The class can then decide which points of view used more reasoning and evidence than others. Based on this activity, the class can discuss connections to larger social issues such as race, class, gender, and other biases. In addition, historical, economic, and global influences can be identified. The purpose is not to determine guilt or a solution but to identify multiple points of view and the complicating factors that facilitate understanding the complexity of a problem.

MINILESSONS ABOUT ARGUMENTATIVE WRITING

Considering Facts, Definitions, Criteria, and Policies

Argumentative writing should involve careful research and deliberation because decisions should never be made from weak assumptions or a narrow bias. In this exercise, writers research an issue related to the people or places important to their projects that are larger than one specific person or place. For instance, the experiences related to one family farm connect to larger national and global economic issues, or a military soldier's service is complicated by a culture's response to a conflict and national budgets. The personal is always political on some level. Students consider the issues that are in the news during the time period of their project or that would interest the people represented in the project. By making connections to larger social issues, writers will help their readers understand the significance of the whole research project.

After researching a selected social issue, writers develop their argument by responding to a series of stasis questions. Originating with Greek and Roman rhetoricians like Cicero, stasis questions can prevent arguments from stalling and becoming ineffective (Herrick, 2005). Writers jot down ideas by responding to four large categories of questions: facts, definitions, criteria, and policy. An example of a criteria question is, *What are the assumptions that different views have in common?* (See http://www.nancymack.me/ for a list of stasis questions for developing an argument.) When prewriting, the point is to generate ideas without judgment so that thoughts build from one another and possibly stimulate unexpected connections. Ideas are always related to other ideas, so even a weak idea may lead a writer to a better one.

When prewriting an argument, writers should examine diverse points of view. A quick way to solicit alternative points of view is to create a walking journal. Based on their brainstormed ideas for the four categories of questions, students free-write a timed journal entry, presenting an argument for an issue connected to the people and places in their projects. Then, the journal is passed to a peer, or writers can switch chairs in a computer lab. Readers respond to the journal entry, commenting on the reasoning and suggesting potential additions. Walking journals should be passed to multiple readers. Students have also enjoyed passing their walking journals to friends and family outside of class to receive additional points of view. Sometimes, a person from a different generation can add contextual information that might be overlooked by the writer. People who disagree aid writers in understanding the viewpoints of others and constructing counterarguments. Understanding the factors that have influenced differing viewpoints leads to coexistence, compromise, or consensus, which can be more advantageous than trying to destroy oppositional viewpoints.

Supporting Reasons with Evidence

Without a clear structure, an impassioned argument can quickly get out of a writer's control. That structure must be clear to both the writer and the reader—especially if the reader is uninterested or influenced by other factors. By learning about claims, reasons, evidence, and warrants, writers can construct a fully developed argument (see Figure 7.1). This type of organizational structure for an argument is adapted from the work of Stephen Toulmin (2003), an academic interested in a practical application of formal logic.

Each type of evidence needs to be presented in a way that makes it easy to accept it as true. For example, facts need to be presented with sources, experts need to have their credentials documented, research methodology needs to be explained, and anecdotes need to be relevant. Sometimes, the warrant is assumed; however, the reader must be able to agree with the assumption. A warrant can be the common ground or the greater good

Figure 7.1. Definitions of Argument Terms

Claim: A claim is a statement that can be researched, questioned, debated, and defended. A claim can dispute a fact, cause, value, or policy. A claim also needs to be specific so it can be supported with more than personal opinion.

Reasons: Reasons provide an explanation for the claim's assertion. Reasons address why the claim is accurate, believable, possible, or true. Reasons are statements that are often linked to a claim with the word *because*.

Evidence: Evidence is the data or grounds that prove a particular reason. Evidence should be verifiable or documented. Types of convincing evidence are facts, expert opinions, research, or anecdotes from personal experience.

Warrant: Warrant is the bridge between the reason and the evidence. Evidence needs to be directly connected to the reason, or the possibility exists that the evidence could be caused by a totally different reason. A warrant is an assumption of what is good or valuable and therefore becomes criteria for judgment.

on which most people can agree. Sometimes warrants are thought of as "if-then" statements with the "if" clause being something that most would affirm or desire.

Students can become familiar with claims, reasons, evidence, and warrants by participating in the following activity before applying the concepts to their own projects. Groups each select a card that lists a ridiculous topic that the group must argue to the whole class. I have used topics like pencils should be banned from schools, every classroom should have a pet cat, classrooms should not have windows, schools should abolish sports, and all students should be required to take a knitting class. Other extreme topics could be related to the local community or popular culture. After each group has a topic, they receive filing cards on which to write down their reasons, evidence, and warrants. Groups must first rewrite their topic as a specific claim and one or two reasons on the board. For example, *Pencils should be banned from school because they are potential weapons and contain harmful chemicals*. After the claim is established, the evidence, and warrants are written on different cards. For each reason to be accepted, the groups should make up evidence such as facts, expert opinions, research, and/or anecdotes. Groups must also reveal a matching warrant or assumed value for each piece of evidence. Groups are given a time limit and present their argument before a "judge" who accepts or rejects any cards presented by a group. The group with the most accepted cards wins.

Although this is meant to be a fun activity for learning terminology associated with creating an effective argument, writers need to develop their reasons fully with evidence. Writers should strive to use more than one type of evidence: facts, expert opinions, research, or anecdotes. Moreover, each of these needs to be explained fully to be convincing. Toulmin's (2003) logic for constructing an argument should not be made into a rigid format; it is more helpful when viewed as a general framework to keep in mind while developing an argument.

MORE STRATEGIES AND ACTIVITIES

Selecting an Argumentative Genre

Many genres utilize argumentative writing. Remember that argumentative, informative, and narrative writing are strategies that can be employed in the same genre. For argumentative writing, students tend to prefer public forums such as newspapers, magazines, blogs, nominations, and proposals. Writers can adopt the point of view of a person important to their project. On the other hand, the argumentative genre can be from the perspective of someone in the general public or a person who holds a different viewpoint. For example, a student who did a project about hospice volunteers included the point of view of a doctor who was against transferring a patient to hospice. Including conflicting points of view in a research project not only adds more drama but also helps to make the whole project more complex and accurate.

Acknowledging Counterarguments

Arguments are put forward when there is some type of communication with an oppositional viewpoint; otherwise, there would be no need for an argument. Effective arguments must include an analysis of the opposition's viewpoint. However, the opposition's viewpoint should not be trivialized or presented as unreasonable. Psychologist Carl Rogers suggests that communication is more effective when trust is built on common ground and threat is reduced (Rogers & Roethlisberger, 1952). In a Rogerian argument, writers avoid confrontation by acknowledging the context in which the opposing viewpoint is valid. From respect for the opposition's viewpoint, the writer searches for points of agreement through empathetic listening and research. For example, understanding the religious beliefs of a family may help find common ground when advocating for the acceptance of a new spouse. In a global community with diverse cultures, it is critical that argumentative writing be more than conquest and conversion (Gearhart, 1979).

To emphasize the importance of respecting other points of view, I ask the class to analyze how counterarguments are presented in a historic document such as Martin Luther King's "Letter from Birmingham City Jail" (Vare & Smith, 2007) First, the class determines King's purpose and how that purpose affects his choice of argumentative style. Then, working in groups, students identify passages where King uses Rogerian strategies by listening to the opposition, seeking common ground, building trust, and reducing threat.

TIPS AND RESOURCES

Keeping a Respectful Tone

Tone is the attitude the author displays about the subject or audience. The tone of writing is created by the examples and word choice or diction that the author employs. Even though a piece of writing may take a stance opposite to the point of view of others, it is unwise for a writer to appear combative, flippant, or condescending. Adopting an offensive tone can destroy a writer's credibility or ethos with the reader. It takes careful word choice to sound reasonable in stressful circumstances. Students should use the thesaurus to tone down words choices like *enemy*, *stupid*, and *wrong*. Likewise, an informal tone can be inappropriate even in email. In public documents or high-stakes situations, writers generally adopt a formal tone. Peers can read one another's drafts to find places to make improvements in tone.

Avoiding Indefinite Pronouns

Note how the next two sentences are confusing: *This is a problem. It is best not to use them this way.* When a writer begins a sentence with an indefinite pronoun such as *it, this, that, these,* or *those,* the reader has to return to the previous sentence or paragraph to figure out the reference. Argumentative writing involves the analysis of complex ideas that need to be clearly explained. Often, the only way to clarify the ideas being discussed is to lengthen the sentence by using the reference noun. For example, the confusing sentences above can be rewritten: *Indefinite pronouns should not be used to start a sentence because the meaning is unclear.* Editing partners can check for sentences that begin with indefinite pronouns.

Even though there are many examples of aggressive argumentation in the media, students need to learn how to present their claims with reasons, evidence, and warrants. Constructing an academic argument requires treating the counterarguments of others in a respectful way rather than escalating the situation into a confrontation. Including narrative, informative, and argumentative writing into one project helps writers understand the usefulness of each. Chapter 8 encourages students to widen their choices for publishing their projects by considering pop-ups, inexpensive scrapbooks, and multimedia.

Publishing with Graphics, Interactive Scrapbooks, and Multimedia

Including graphics in a writing project can increase student motivation and enhance the entire composing process. In the early stages of drafting, I ask for a show of hands to see how many writers are already imagining what they want their finished project to look like. Most indicate that they have already begun visualizing potential images, layouts, and/or media they will use. This feedback has convinced me that the use of images can be an important component for conceptualizing meaning rather than simply a decorative afterthought.

Brain research tells us that images are central to all symbol-making practices whether we are drawing, speaking, or writing. Jody Murray (2009), a composition scholar, explains how thought is conceived from connections being made among images, language, and emotions. Murray cites the work of neuroscientists Antonio R. Damasio (1999), Steven Pinker (1997), and Vilayanur Ramachandran and Sandra Blakeslee (1998) to explain that image is the building block of language and consciousness. One poignant image can provoke the recall of many rich memories that would take hundreds of words to express. Kristine Fleckenstein, an expert on visual literacy, argues that image is less static and more of a process that is essential to the language arts classroom for both reading and writing (Fleckenstein, Calendrillo, & Worley, 2002).

Having used publication projects with middle and high school students before I started teaching in prison, I knew that graphic projects motivate disengaged writers. However, I was not so sure the same would be true for adult male repeat offenders. I decided to take a risk with one student, who was in solitary confinement for stabbing another inmate, to test the response. I sent instructions for the inmate to write an essay about an issue of conflict in prison and to present it artistically on a large piece of poster board. As might be expected, the inmate in question was pretty hostile and angry in the few weeks he had been in class prior to his confinement; therefore, I never really expected him to complete the assignment. Low and behold, he was released from solitary during the final exam in time to turn in his project. Most of the class was writing silently when the inmate came through the doorway. Instantly, a rumble began to roll through the room, and I feared that this inmate had generated enough hostility to cause a fight to break out. I stood up and demanded to be told what the problem was. A spokesperson for the rest of the class explained how unfair it was for the inmate who was in solitary confinement to have been given the privilege of doing a special project. Dumbfounded, I asked if they wanted to do graphic projects with their own essays, to which the answer was an incredulous positive response from everyone. From this and other experiences I have learned that any age or type of writer has the potential to enjoy a writing assignment that incorporates graphics.

When graphics are an essential component to the message, projects can inspire higher-quality writing. The inmate from the previous example wrote about how the men in prison are just pawns in the prison system's racist games. The essay extended the metaphor with examples about how Black prisoners were treated by various types of guards. The graphic was a red and black chessboard with a prisoner as a pawn, wearing a man's face divided in two, half Black and half White. The inmate explained that he had searched numerous newspapers in order to find two matching faces just the right size to tear out for the chess pawn. To complete my story, I promised the class that they would all get to make this type of project the following term. Some of the projects the inmates created from trash they recycled within the prison included a picture of a television with a rotating wheel behind a clear screen, a cardboard and tape sculpture of a pay telephone, a 3-D cardboard fuse box, and a boom box replica with an essay that pulled out on a rolling window-shade mechanism. Since my early attempts at incorporating graphics, I have been blown away by the quality of writing in these graphic projects. Mind you, not every project has been clever, beautiful, or closely connected to excellent writing, but the vast majority has been stunning.

Respecting the learning style differences of the students means that it is important to consider as many media as possible. Writers can experiment with publishing one genre or the whole project with digital media. The Common Core State Standards encourage the use of technology and the Internet. Computer-generated graphics and multimedia web platforms have changed how we communicate in daily life. Not only are visual images enhancing classroom instruction, graphic presentations like PowerPoint and podcasts have become a staple for businesses to present new ideas to clients and the public. Thinking and communicating in images will only grow in importance in the future as we carry multimedia wherever we go with our phones and other mobile devices. However, the increase in digital technology has not diminished our interest in hand-crafting items (Crawford, 2015). Making scrapbooks has become a popular way for families to preserve their memoires. Making simple pop-ups delights students of all ages.

In fact, when our daughter was a substitute teacher, she would show a pop-up that students would be able to make at the end of the day as a reward for good behavior. Most students are surprised that pop-ups are so easy to make. Writers should start with whatever graphic skills they possess and then stretch themselves by experimenting with at least one medium that is new to them.

This chapter suggests several ways for students to become familiar with the many choices available for publishing individual genres as well as the whole project. Explanations are included for inexpensive paper-bag scrapbooks and interactive page elements. Overviews are provided for digital still and animated multimedia formats. Visual metaphors can be brainstormed to encourage the thematic use of graphics as symbols.

MOTIVATORS AND INSPIRATIONS

Considering Different Types of Publishing

To provide a starting place for writers thinking about publishing options, I show examples of the different media that previous students have used for their projects. (See http://www.nancymack.me/ for photographs of projects.) The class can make a list of the types of projects to consider, including physical projects such as scrapbooks, paper-bag books, and cardboard boxes, and digital projects such as blogs, websites, slide presentations, podcasts, movies, comics, and animated cartoons.

Examining Moveable Parts in Picture Books

To generate ideas for adding interactive elements to print projects, I recommend sharing picture books with moveable parts, especially books with pockets, envelopes, flaps, fold-outs, partial pages, transparent pages, wheels, pull-outs, and pop-ups. Students can examine these more closely when motivation is lagging. (See http://www.nancymack.me/ for a bibliography of books with moveable parts.)

Making a Simple Pop-Up

Students love making simple pop-ups such as a step pop-up or an information wheel. Many step-by-step directions and videos can be found online. Joan Irvine's book *How to Make Pop-Ups* is one of the easiest to follow (Irvine & Reid, 1987). (My books about teaching grammar with poetry contain directions for making pop-ups and other types of publishing [Mack 2005, 2008].)

Viewing Mark Twain's Scrapbook

For an historical view of scrapbooking, several archival photographs of Mark Twain's scrapbooks can be found on the Internet, including his invention of self-pasting pages. Students can consider how the visual artifacts relate to Twain's essays about his travels. Scrapbooks were popular in the 1800s. Liz Rohan (2004) has studied how fears about the limits of memory during this era prompted people to keep scrapbooks and photographs in order to preserve important ties to deceased loved ones.

MINILESSONS ABOUT PUBLISHING

Making a Paper-Bag Scrapbook

Recycling helps keep the costs down for creating multigenre projects. Students have used cereal boxes, pizza boxes, and pocket folders to house their projects; but the most popular means for publishing physical projects has been paper-bag books. Large brown paper grocery bags are incredibly strong. Decorative paper can be glued to pages, and the side pockets can hold regular-sized paper. Some creative students have even cut flaps in the bottom portion of the bag to reveal graphics, letters, and small objects. (For examples of paper-bag scrapbooks, see Figures 8.1 and 8.2 as well as http://www.nancymack.me/, which also includes directions for making a paper bag scrapbook.)

Choosing Digital Media

Computer programs and web platforms have made it possible for individual writers to produce sophisticated multimedia. However, students need to be sure to estimate their computer abilities as well as the time they have available. Several of my students have created websites to house their whole multigenre project. Former student Eileen Williamson wrote about her Texas high school drill team and created an interactive website to gather stories and photographs from several decades. The site became so popular that she later moved it to a Facebook group. Lori Sorrels, also a student, created a PowerPoint project about her father's love of building small planes. Lori embedded her genres on individual slides that featured photographs and graphics.

Publishing one genre using digital media may be more realistic than developing a large website or huge multimedia production. Newer web platforms change frequently and may require students to create accounts and pay for special features. To help writers become familiar with current

Figure 8.1. Janie Freund's Paper-Bag Scrapbook About Her Father, an Air Force First Responder

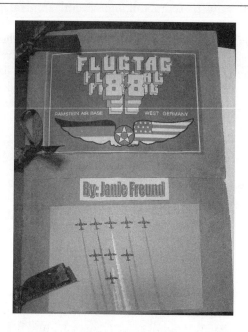

Figure 8.2. Inside Janie Freund's Paper-Bag Scrapbook

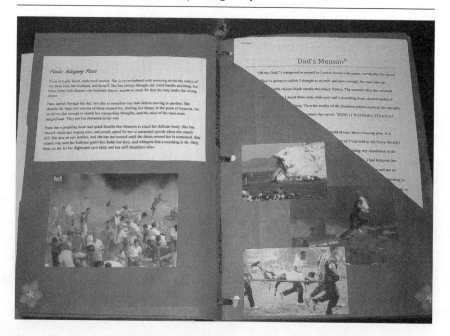

multimedia, I ask the class to make a list of available digital graphic, audio, and video formats (see Figure 8.3). Then I poll the class to find out which multimedia platforms students know how to use. Then mentors can volunteer who are willing to demonstrate how to use new media programs or websites.

Figure 8.3. Multimedia for Publishing Genres

- Facebook pages can include posts, photographs, notes, and a timeline
- Blogs from websites such as Blogger, Tumblr, WordPress, Blog, LiveJournal, or SquareSpace
- Wikis including Weebly, PB Works, Simplebooklet, or Google Sites
- Infographics like Piktochart
- Slide presentations such as PowerPoint and Prezi
- Video slide shows like Animoto
- Digital comics like Pixton
- Animated cartoons like Xtranormal
- Audio sound tracks
- Podcasts
- Digital movies

Publishing digital media can include various options. A single digital genre can be burned onto a CD, saved onto a USB flash drive, or printed out and combined with a paper project. Envelopes or pockets can be glued to a page to hold discs or drives. The digital contents should be annotated on a slip of paper for ease of reference. Including a hard copy of the digital genre is suggested in case the data are lost or corrupted. In some cases, this can be done with features such as PowerPoint handouts or by printing a screen shot. Writers should always try to save data in two different places—for instance, in an email or a cloud site such as Dropbox. When in doubt about how to publish with digital media, a student should check with the teacher or the media support staff first. Larger digital files can be zipped or uploaded to websites such as Slide Share or YouTube. For an entirely digital project, all genres can be embedded into a slide presentation, Facebook page, or wiki website, but remember that some host websites require Internet access in order to view the project.

MORE STRATEGIES AND ACTIVITIES

Publishing with Recycled Folders, Boxes, and Other Containers

Pocket file folders can be attached together to hold hard copies of different genres. Student Ellen Gilbert, who wrote about the history of a local train station, glued pictures of train cars to the fronts of the pockets and incorporated a timeline on the folder above each pocket. Adapting boxes of all types has also become popular. Ryan Hudgins, also a student, attached paper-bag pages with brads to the inside of a pizza box to create a scrapbook (see Figure 8.4). Another student covered a cereal box to look like a striped popcorn bag that held all the genres about a historic movie theater.

Writers have made time capsules from cylindrical-shaped chip cans and have recycled boxes and bags to look like suitcases and purses. If the genres are loose inside a container, they need to be numbered in the order in which they are supposed to be read.

Figure 8.4. Ryan Hudgins's Multigenre Project in a Pizza Box About an Incident at a Restaurant

Brainstorming Visual Metaphors

Brainstorming visual metaphors can help writers who are less likely to enjoy using visuals in their project or have fewer resources for creating graphics. After brainstorming alone, students should share ideas in pairs or small groups to provide more ideas for graphics. One image that has a symbolic connection to the central theme of the project can be repeated throughout to create unity. For example, student Rachel Howell Cornett featured a lit candle throughout a project about Rankin House to symbolize its role in the Underground Railroad. Because many writers choose topics about family members in the military, flags and other military symbols can be placed in blank spaces. These types of symbols are easily found by searching images on the Internet and provide an inexpensive way to incorporate graphics into a project. Before they incorporate graphics into their projects, I have found that writers benefit from discussing graphic design concepts of color, balance, repetition, dominance, and eye movement. These concepts can be illustrated with graphics from published sources such as book covers.

TIPS AND RESOURCES

Using Graphics and Artifacts During Interviews

When interviewing adults about experiences that took place many years ago, looking at objects or photographs can stimulate memories. For example, one student printed out pictures of housewives and kitchens from the 1950s to help her mother remember small details about participating in a Pillsbury Bake-Off contest. Images of clothing, furnishings, cars, or advertisements from the decade of the event can visually tap into long-forgotten memories and can later be added to the project.

Creating Interactive Page Elements

Readers enjoy items that can be added to a paper project that will make it more interactive. A small feature such as a turning Fact Wheel made with a brad gives a project extra appeal (see Chapter 2). Envelopes glued to a page can hold letters, and a sealed envelope cut in half makes an ideal pocket for holding a brochure or small booklet. Large business envelopes, sealed with one end cut open, can be glued to the back of a page to hold a pull-out feature. (See http://www.nancymack.me/ for a list of interactive page elements and directions for creating aged paper.)

Students need to see a wide range of creative possibilities in order to find a favorite publishing idea for their projects. Multimedia and paper-crafting have generated great interest in multigenre writing from students, teachers, and audiences. Recycled and low-cost paper-crafting has become an unexpected hit among my students. Chapter 9 focuses on different types of project feedback from the celebration of finished masterpieces to proofreading, assessment, and self-reflection.

Encouraging Feedback, Reflection, Assessment, and Celebration

When I first started assigning multigenre projects, I was a little concerned that colleagues might think the projects were more artistic than academic. To counter this misconception, I arrived early at a faculty meeting and plopped down a stack of projects in the middle of the table. A senior colleague, who had authored a textbook on writing research papers, picked up a project and started reading it. The student's project was about her father's experiences during the Vietnam War—an experience that my colleague shared. Not only was he impressed with the writing; he was pleased with the explanatory endnotes. I have found that my students' excellent projects speak for themselves. Some may still have minor typos and usage errors, but the power of the writing makes almost every project a treasure.

Positive attitudes are important for our lives both inside and outside of the classroom. I decided a few years ago that if I dreaded reading a set of student papers, then I needed to rethink the assignment to make it more interesting for both the students and myself. Sharing student work as good examples demonstrates a teacher's genuine joy and respect for what students write. In an essay entitled "In Praise of Praise," Paul Diederich (2006), an early expert on assessment, wrote about his favorite writing teacher who began class by reading examples of what students did well rather than reporting on how horrendous the errors were in their last efforts. Of course, effusive praise can be ingenuous and even harmful. Sam Dragga (1988) has done empirical research about praiseworthy comments on students' writing and points out that praise needs to be focused and specific. Writers may indeed do something well and be unaware of the technique that they employed.

As a beginning teacher, I felt guilty if I did not circle every error on students' papers. I call this the Lady Macbeth theory of error: "Out, out damn spot." It would be wonderful if drawing circles around errors made them go away. The worst effects of marking for error in the traditional way are that it eats up the teacher's time outside of the class, and students largely ignore and misunderstand the comments the teacher makes on their papers (Montgomery, 2009).

Teaching takes much more effort than drawing circles around errors, and in order for students to learn new features of language, direct instruction is necessary. When teaching about error, students first need to have their attention drawn to what was good in a correct example. Commercial skill-builders are too full of incorrect examples that are not brain-compatible for learning. Teaching from incorrect examples would be like showing a math problem with the wrong answer and telling students to infer how to work the problem correctly from it. The effect of using correct models was powerfully demonstrated to me by a student who insisted that he had punctuated a compound sentence correctly when he put a comma behind the "and" rather than in front of it. He explained that he had punctuated his sentence the same way that I had written it on the board: *When joining two sentences, put the comma in front of the and, but, or, nor, for, so, or yet.* The visual cues were the opposite of the intended meaning. Errors can be based on conflicting visual or auditory examples. Many of us have made errors because of conflicts with dialect and vernacular language.

Positive support is important when students are learning a new language feature. My father's theory of learning was that most mistakes were not stupid—they are just a matter of working from the wrong theory about things. For example, when I did a study of my 8th-grade students' sentence fragments, I discovered that most of them were actually subordinate clauses. Students sensed that the subordinate clauses were a unit, so they punctuated the fragments like a sentence. They just did not know how to attach those units to either the sentence before or after the fragment. Fragment errors were an interim stage in learning to write complex sentences. Talking about why we do things one way and why another way is preferred helps students make sense of many of the confusing aspects of the English language. Even then, we need to be gentle with learners as they try a new approach and make more mistakes along the way.

This chapter includes suggestions for sharing multigenre projects both inside and outside the classroom. It features assessment, including commenting on drafts and creating interactive grade sheets. The important topics of proofreading and minimal marking are explained. Metacognitive reflection is encouraged through having students write a preface essay and also giving feedback to the teacher at the end of the project.

MOTIVATORS AND INSPIRATIONS

Sharing Finished Projects

Sharing folklore projects with the class has many benefits for everyone involved. Hearing writers talk about their projects always gives me new insights about students and their writing processes and primes me to look forward to reading their work. For the students, sharing provides an opportunity to reflect on the process, point out their favorite aspects of their project, and bask in the glory of all their hard work. For the class, sharing is a powerful bonding experience in which we learn to respect important parts of one another's lives. Because students write about meaningful people and places, writers and listeners sometimes cry or laugh out loud during sharing. I have always felt fortunate that students are comfortable sharing their personal reactions with the class. Therefore, I leave it up to the class if they want to invite guests.

Planning a Community Event

Once a year, my university has a Language Arts Fair to celebrate the writing of local college, high school, and middle school students. Teachers, administrators, and families come to enjoy the creativity of their students. Display tables are full of scrapbook, box, and other physical multigenre projects, including those of my students. Teachers explain their assignments and introduce their students, who describe their projects. Visitors then move to a computer classroom to view students' amazing websites, slide shows, and movies. Afterward, everyone listens to a reading by a local published author. This type of event is worth all the time and effort required to plan it. Several universities across the country have also adopted multigenre research writing and are holding yearly celebrations. Celebration rather than competition should be the reason for sharing students' projects.

MINILESSONS ABOUT COMPLETING THE PROJECT

Giving Feedback on Drafts

As mentioned in Chapter 4, I only comment on second drafts. Before that stage, I present minilessons about specific topics, followed by guided in-class revision on first drafts and continued with more out-of-class revision time. I respond quickly to second drafts of longer genres with highlighting and minimal comments. Three colors are used for highlighting with a key posted at the top of each returned draft. Green highlighting is used for text that is interesting or good, yellow is for text that needs minor revision, and pink is for major revision. I now prefer responding electronically, but I started out using highlighting markers on paper drafts. I restrict my checking to the topics that were covered in the minilessons so that I do not highlight for everything. When I add comments, I do so in purple ink or font. Positive comments are specific, pointing out the strategy or device that the student did well. Negative comments are phrased as "opportunities" to add more of what was demonstrated in the minilesson. For instance, I often write *An opportunity for sensory details to make the reader feel present in the scene.* Specific suggestions are offered as a choice between two possibilities. For example, I might write *This genre could begin with the action that happens in the third paragraph*, or *A scene by the side of the road could be added to the opening.*

I find that this system of formative assessment for revision is quick, and students tend to make bigger changes than they do with any other system that I have tried. Students tell me they like the highlighting because it is easy to see and understand. The type and amount of highlighting and commenting is varied for each student's needs. For instance, an excellent draft may receive more yellow than pink highlighting but would certainly receive some suggestions for improvement. Highlighting helps me see if I am taking over the student's paper by making too many suggestions. (For more information about this practice, see Mack, 2013.)

Prewriting the Project Preface

A preface at the beginning of a volume prepares the reader for the text that follows by explaining how and why the work was created. Students write a preface near the end of the process, when they know which genres they will include. In order to be sure that writers discuss all the information required, I give prompts one at a time for a series of 2-minute free-writes (see Figure 9.1). These free-writes give writers a good start on a finished preface.

Figure 9.1. Prompts for the Preface or Cover Letter

Tell why you selected this topic and a particular person to interview.

Explain the particular strategies that you used to research academic sources for your project and in what ways these sources added to your understanding of the topic.

Describe your efforts to accurately and ethically represent the people, places, and events in your project. Give specific examples of any problems that you had and/or the decisions you made.

Give specific details about your writing process and what you learned about writing by doing this project. Include examples of how your drafts or the project changed during the process.

Describe your use of multiple dialects and registers in your genres. Tell your reasons for including formal language in some genres and dialect in others.

Tell why these stories about real people and places are important to you and why this information should be important to the university and society at large.

As can be seen by the prompts, I prefer for student prefaces to contain a lot of information about the completed project as well as the process of creating the project from beginning to end. I value the fact that the preface demonstrates a critical analysis of the content and a reflection about the writing process and language use.

Proofreading for Marks Rather Than Meaning

Proofreading is a completely different type of reading. I prove this to students by first giving them a speed-reading test. After telling students they will only have a few seconds to read a sentence silently, I flash a sentence that contains minor errors such as missing vowels, repeated words, and missing plurals on a screen. Most readers notice very few errors because good readers visually skip letters and whole words. All readers predict meaning from just a few visual clues.

Reading for meaning is totally different from reading for errors. Reading for errors requires readers to read for the tiny marks on the page. This is especially difficult because writers often see what they want to see in their work, even if it is not really there. Thus, people who are strangers to the content can find more errors in the writing than the author. Moreover, proofreading for dots and dots with tails is extremely boring; consequently, the brain actually resists proofreading, so much so that good proofreaders develop strategies to trick their brains into not reading for meaning (Harris, 1987). One effective method is to read the paper out loud to slow down the brain in order to see errors. To spot run-ons and fragments, read the paper from the last sentence forward, one sentence at a time. Reading the paper from the last sentence forward prevents reading for meaning. Some proofreaders find it helpful to slide a filing card or a ruler along the lines of the text to prevent their eyes from moving too quickly.

MORE STRATEGIES AND ACTIVITIES

Editing with Minimal Marking

Minimal marking is an effective strategy that Richard Haswell (1983) has researched, and many writing teachers endorse. Basically, the teacher reads a paper quickly for sentence-level errors, usually only for errors in spelling, punctuation, and usage. A checkmark or X is placed in the margin of each line that contains an error; two marks are used if there are two errors and so on. Minimal marking works with peer partners, too. Partners proofread from the last sentence of the paper forward and put an X in the margin. Only the author is permitted to make changes in the text. Student proofreaders can call the teacher over if they are not sure about an error. This process often results in some interesting questions and spontaneous minilessons.

As noted, only three or four types of errors are marked. The teacher should present a minilesson on the types of errors that were marked before the papers are passed back to the owners. Students are given class time to correct their errors before the papers are graded. The teacher then collects the papers and comments on any corrections that were not made or were made incorrectly. Students report that minimal marking improves their attitudes about errors. If the teacher corrects the errors for them, then students only learn that the teacher is a good proofreader. If they correct their own errors, then the students learn that they can proofread their own papers.

For students who have major problems with errors that are affecting their grades in all their classes, I work one-on-one with minimal marking, having students talk through their search for errors on the marked line. Insights can be gained about what the student is or is not looking for. University writing centers are a great place to go for this type of help. All writers benefit from knowing which types of errors are their personal demons in order to proofread for those errors. Nobody is perfect, not even English teachers.

Using Interactive Grade Sheets

I have been experimenting with interactive grade sheets for the final grading of the multigenre projects. I use a primary trait grade sheet that specifies all the requirements for the project. I have begun adding places on the sheet for students to write in which genre in their project best demonstrates a particular outcome. For instance, if sensory writing is targeted, the author indicates to me which genre has the best sensory writing. I always ask writers to identify which genre contains direct quotes from their academic research. By listing their genre with the best examples of a targeted skill, writers are performing a quick self-assessment. Of course, passing out this sheet early in the process helps writers to be aware of the goals. While grading, I check off the requirements and rank them as exceptional, good, or needing improvement. I always write a personal note to the student about the topic of the project. I have a separate sheet that lists all the process points that were stamped during work on the project, and are quickly tallied. Because I give points all during the term, I count the points as a percentage of students' course grade rather than factoring them into the grade for the multigenre project. (See http://www.nancymack.me/ for an example interactive grade sheet and process points sheet.)

TIPS AND RESOURCES

Wording Comments for Revision

Generally, teachers make too many comments on student papers. The pronouns used in comments can be offensive to writers. The most confrontational pronoun is *you*, and it should be avoided; comments are about a draft and not the worth of the person. Comments should start with *This paper has*. . . . Passive voice is less aggressive, as in *This paper needs proofreading* rather than *You need to proofread this paper*. Comments using first person can be a rhetorical move to make the writer aware that the reader is having problems. So, instead of *Transition needed here* a more effective comment would be *I need help seeing the connection between these two paragraphs*. The second comment is also more specific and thus more helpful to the writer. The best comments just narrate the experience of being a naïve reader. Writers need to be able to imagine someone reading their texts, so mentioning "a reader" depersonalizes the comment from being about one person disliking their writing. In sum, give a few specific comments about problems using *this paper* rather than *you*, and use "I" or "a reader" statements to explain problems in structure and organization. Generally, fewer comments gain more response than many, which tend to overwhelm a writer.

Planning for Oral Presentations

Presentations can be formal or informal. In a quick informal sharing, students explain their topic choice, describe their favorite genre, show one interesting element, and tell one insight they gained from researching and writing about their topic. For formal presentations, students prefer to work from a PowerPoint in which the slides provide organization. Students can go into more detail about their decisions for selecting particular genres and transitions. As an alternative, students can review their projects from beginning to end, showing the genres they composed. Presenters need to be reminded to speak loudly and make eye contact with their audience. Planning time after each presentation for questions is always a good idea.

Encouraging Metacognitive Reflection

At the end of every project or unit, feedback from students should be collected about instructional strategies. Student feedback helps the teacher know what worked and why it was helpful as well as garner suggestions about how to better support students' learning. In providing feedback, students are also engaging in self-assessment about which prewriting, drafting, revising, and proofreading strategies were the most effective. To solicit student feedback, I list all the activities we did and ask students to free-write about several of their favorite strategies, elaborating on the reasons why they were effective. I also ask the following general questions about their learning experience of researching and writing about their topic:

- What did you learn about prewriting from doing this project?
- What did you learn about writing in different genres?
- What did you gain from focusing your project on the folklore stories of real people?
- What did you learn about research and quoting sources?

Many of the students' suggestions have improved the whole project process as well as individual lessons. I continually learn about teaching from my students.

I enjoy celebrating students' accomplishments with audiences outside the classroom whenever possible. I have learned that I must be very careful how I respond to drafts for revision and proofreading so that students do not get discouraged and learn how to improve their own writing without teachers in the future. Most of all, I have learned that multigenre research projects make writing more joyous and meaningful for both writers and readers. Chapter 10 is filled with suggestions for adapting this assignment for various purposes, content areas, grade levels, and curricular standards.

Adapting for Different Contents, Abilities, and Standards

Many of the strategies I present in this book are the result of collaboration with other teachers and students. These innovative strategies have been tweaked, refined, and enjoyed by many colleagues. I never hesitate to give ideas away because teachers always innovate and develop them into even better teaching strategies. Teachers immediately start planning how to adjust the strategy for their particular context, and when I see them again, they tell me more about what their students did and how the strategy was modified again. Of course, some ideas get tossed aside while others, like the "I Am From" poem (see Chapter 5), have seen so many adaptations that they take on a life of their own. What I learned from these experiences is that good teaching practices can be effectively modified for almost any grade and content level. Multigenre writing is an extremely flexible base for the study of almost any content area and motivates students to engage in research.

Of course, I have also seen wonderful teaching strategies stripped of their potential when they become separated from their guiding theories of language and learning. To be honest, I have ruined some classroom strategies myself by being either too controlling or too nondirective. Occasionally, I even trash an assignment because it has become too much of a routine. My learning is a form of teacher research through which I seek solutions for problems that arise as well as the principles that provoke unexpected successes. Sometimes, the success of a teaching strategy or assignment is the most puzzling to me. If I cannot understand what learning theories are implicated, the success of one assignment will fade away and never happen again or will only happen for a limited circumstance. The wonderful success of multigenre writing has captivated my attention for many years of research and development.

This chapter contains ideas for adapting multigenre research writing for several subject contents, grade levels, and standards. Former students who are now wonderful teachers developed the majority of these adaptations. The study of a novel can be extended into an examination of relevant social issues. Combining history, science, sociology, or other academic subjects with nontraditional genres increase students' interest in research. In other classrooms, teachers have employed multiple genres for reports about future careers and plans for college. Important standards, difficult skills, and new media can all be incorporated in a larger multigenre project that is not limited to one traditional school genre. Grade-level examples span from middle through graduate school. A chart is included in the appendix that indexes the Common Core Standards with all the minilessons and activities in this book.

LINKING OTHER CURRICULAR CONTENT AREAS

One of the most exciting types of multigenre projects centers on a novel and involves analysis and connections to related social issues. Almost every novel has a character who experiences a major problem, as illustrated by the following two examples. Shelly Poeppelman had her high school students each select a book that addressed issues such as poverty in Jeanette Walls's *Glass Castle* (2005), the treatment of Afghan women in Khaled Hosseini's *A Thousand Splendid Suns* (2007), or child soldiers in Ishmael Beah's *A Long Way Gone* (2007). After discussing potential social issues in literature circles, students selected a research topic and published their results in a creative multigenre project. For example, some students studied China's one-child law, others personally connected with researching the effect of GMOs on children with asthma, and one investigated the impact Barbie has on self-image. Students invented a new scene for the novel, including anything from birth certificates and passports to stream of consciousness writing—all of which was supported with research in the endnotes. At another school, teacher Kristen Race utilized multigenre projects to help her students find common ground in difficult multicultural texts. Students explored the cultural concepts in *Things Fall Apart* (Achebe, 1994) through collage, music, dance, poetry, essay, playwriting, and so forth. For example, one student rewrote the scene of Ikemefuna's death, taught the class an Igbo dance, and wrote a creative nonfiction piece about food staples in the character's family.

Social issues have an important place in the content of many college courses. For a women's studies course, Jill Channing assigned students to complete multigenre projects focusing on a significant aspect of female family members' lives. Examining gender and social class conflicts is more dynamic when writers interview family members about their experiences. For example, one student wrote about a relative's long employment as a seamstress in a shirt factory, and another represented a woman's conflict with her wealthy mother-in-law. In the conclusion to their projects, some students chose to analyze the traits they shared with their relatives, such as the strength and determination to face hard times and difficult experiences. In a thematic composition course, Don Bruce asked his students to tackle difficult social issues such as bullying and poverty by observing how different groups deal with conflict. After analyzing three different groups, students created posters, surveys, short stories, comics, wanted posters, poems, and videos to represent their views about a social issue.

Multigenre projects can inspire students to research historical connections that enrich their understanding of novels. Meagan Wagner was impressed that her high school students not only researched historical information about World War II when they read *Night* by Elie Wiesel (2006), but they also found personal connections with their families' wartime histories. One student generated letters, postcards, and even packages from home that re-created his family's experiences. Others supplemented their multigenre projects with artifacts that family members had saved from a relative's military service. In a career and technical school, Niki Patton created an entire unit about the Vietnam War to teach her students to write for various purposes and audiences. Students learned basic research skills such as evaluating the credibility of sources by reading reference materials, scholarly journals, and articles from magazines about subjects such as U.S. involvement in the war as well as post-traumatic stress disorder. They read poetry by Vietnam War veterans, excerpts from Tim O'Brien's *The Things They Carried* (1998), and listened to music from the era. Students responded to photographs by writing poetry, letters, and short stories from the perspective of soldiers. In addition, they wrote newspaper articles and quizzes about the war, and they designed war propaganda and protest posters. Finally, the projects were assembled and displayed in creative ways. For instance, one student created a tombstone for a soldier that opened up to hold all the genres she had written. Another student used an authentic rucksack to hold her writings. Patton believes this project enabled her students to be more cognitively engaged and motivated to write than they had been all year—not to mention that the writing was indeed the best she had seen from her students.

On the college level, a historical approach to literature can be extended into sophisticated critical analysis. Michelle Wood had her Cedarville University students select a novel and analyze its theme from a New Historical and Bahktinian perspective and present that analysis in a multigenre project. Multigenre writing enabled her students to understand, analyze, and represent the multiple voices that informed not only the discourses in the novel but also the historical and social realities that produced it. One student focused on the theme of Justice in *Billy Budd* (Melville, 1990) and another wrote a musical composition from the perspective of an Irish immigrant whom Thoreau discusses meeting in *Walden* (1971).

In addition to history, science content can be integrated into multigenre writing. Middle school science teacher Jennifer Beeghly has used various genres for students to report on ecosystems such as an "I Am From" poem from a piranha's point of view. A chemistry teacher assigned students to create a character for different elements of the periodic table to demonstrate the element's traits through writing creative genres such as medieval diary entries from a woman dying of lead poisoning. Multigenre projects can be part of an interdisciplinary unit in which students write different genres for different content areas. In collaboration with Jenn Reid at the Dayton Regional STEM School, Beth Fullenkamp-Jansen based a cross-curricular unit on two novels about cancer: *The Fault in Our Stars* (Green, 2012) and *My Sister's Keeper* (Picoult, 2004). For biology class, students researched the disease; for health class, they studied lifestyle habits to avoid cancer; and for English class, they wrote a story following the progression of a character's experience with a cancer diagnosis. At another high school, Lindsay Williams wanted her students to have an investment in the fight against cancer, so she arranged for them to visit a cancer research lab as well as interview teenagers who described what it's like to experience the disease firsthand. In addition, the students were able to conduct a question-and-answer session with the parent of a cancer survivor in order to get another perspective. Students then chose different types of cancer and collaborated on reports with visuals and other genres.

CONNECTING TO COMMUNITIES

Encouraging students to select project topics connected to local communities can prevent them from gravitating toward hackneyed topics and can even result in service-learning opportunities. Stephie Fannin and Lisa Bakita devised a multigenre project for middle school students with the theme of heroes. In several genres, many students chose to honor family members who served in the military, resulting in a local newspaper article about the project for Veterans Day. Lisa Bakita also had her students research and write about community organizations where many later did volunteer work.

My colleague David Seitz (2014) has written about a college composition course with the theme of place that focuses on a critical rhetorical analysis of change within a local community. Students selected a neighborhood, town, or workplace and researched community bonds, local history, and global influences. Then, they composed several genres based upon personal experience, interviews, and academic sources. For example, one student wrote about the decision to move a large local industry out of state, another wrote about the efforts of a rural town to revitalize the downtown during a recession in the global economy, and another analyzed the power relations among small fellowship churches compared with the greater anonymity of megachurch models.

Jacqueline Preston (2015) explains how she and her colleagues use multigenre writing with college composition students in conjunction with project-based learning. Students used multiple genres to dramatize topics, explore problems, and design community service projects. Their projects included short stories that zero in on a memorable event and help identify related topics of interest. Students used their short stories as springboards for producing a radio essay for NPR, which required them to attend to a particular audience and extend a personal issue to one of larger political or social relevance. As part of their research, students wrote interview protocols, which provoked students to ask questions designed to challenge their assumptions. Next, students proposed solutions to social, academic, or workplace problems they had identified through their research. Proposals addressed issues such as preventing diabetes, strengthening the local bike culture, developing persuasion skills in children, supporting mothers returning to school, and understanding children and grief. To supplement their proposals, students created multimodal genres, including brochures, websites, Prezis, and posters that address a need in a concrete way. At the heart of Preston's pedagogy is a focus on writing for a real context and understanding how various genres and mediums connect and support meaning.

FEATURING IMPORTANT STANDARDS AND SKILLS

Professional teachers always consult state and district curricula, standards, and outcomes when they create daily lesson plans. Posting and discussing each day's standards and objectives center classroom activities and reinforce their purpose. Thus, students can be aware of both what and how they are learning. Teachers find that multigenre projects can incorporate specific standards and state mandates, thus making planning and assessment much easier. Multigenre research projects provide a flexible platform to integrate many of the Common Core State Standards that otherwise would be covered in isolated, stand-alone lessons.

The CCSS for writing are organized around three text modes—specifically, argumentative, informative, and narrative writing. By including all three of these text types in one project, students learn how specific genres use rhetorical strategies for different purposes (see Chapters 4, 6, and 7). For example, Katina Childers designed a multigenre unit that featured the three modes of writing in the CCSS. She had groups of middle school students create an alien universe in which they wrote informative pieces about their planets and species, family structures, governments, weapons, religions, economic systems, and so forth. They created narratives about their origin myths and odes to their heroes. They used argumentative writing to declare war and eventually create a peace agreement to save their citizens.

The Common Core Standards emphasize nonfiction. Multigenre research projects give teachers two ways to incorporate more nonfiction reading into their curriculum—as both textual evidence and genre models for writing. The CCSS that emphasize close reading and understanding key ideas and specific details in texts are essential when learning to quote academic texts (see Chapters 2 and 6). Likewise, quotes from literary texts are incorporated as thematic transitions between genres (see Chapter 3). The CCSS for examining the craft and structure in texts are linked to brain compatible exercises in genre imitation. Not only is this method of imitation effective for nonfiction texts, but it also is effective for developing character, setting, plot, and theme for genres such as narrative stories, allegories, and fairytales (see Chapters 4 and 5). For both nonfiction and fiction readings, the CCSS suggest comparing and contrasting texts. Genre analysis is a system that helps students move beyond comprehension to study rhetorical features by analyzing and comparing texts to enhance their writing (see Chapter 3).

For any research project to be successful, the topic chosen needs to be carefully selected to build from students' existing knowledge as well as connect to academic sources (see Chapter 1). With the increased emphasis on research in the CCSS, teachers need resources to provide students with a step-by-step approach to find, select, and evaluate academic sources and then comprehend, introduce, cite, and elaborate upon quotes from those sources. Multigenre research projects feature a more realistic use of citation by having students compose nonfiction genres such as newspaper stories, magazine articles, textbook entries, award nominations, proposals, self-help columns, and social worker reports (see Chapter 6).

Some of the CCSS are more difficult for teachers to work into their lesson plans. For instance, the inclusion of historic documents at first seems more appropriate for social studies courses than for English. However, students can study the rhetorical features of famous documents, connecting these examples to the genres students are writing (see Chapters 3 and 7). Regarding the CCSS promotion of technology, some teachers may not have access to computers for every student. Multigenre writing projects can both adapt to limited technology availability as well as the rapid development of new media. Multigenre projects permit advanced students to show off technological skills that may be unfamiliar to others (see Chapter 8). Of course, proofreading is always a difficult skill to teach at every grade level and should be taught as a specific type of reading, different from reading for meaning (see Chapter 9).

In my state, there is currently an emphasis on career and college readiness for high school students. Therefore, Kaytee McBride collaborated with Bambi Osswald to plan a multigenre career exploration project for high school students. Students researched and wrote about a chosen career through multiple voices and perspectives. Garth Mcloed assigned his rural students to research, select, and argue for the college that they wished to attend to their parents, most of whom had never attended college. Some students created websites about their decisionmaking process, and others designed college mailings with personalized information about their choices.

Graduate courses benefit from using multiple genres to acquaint students with difficult content. I teach a graduate course in which students are expected to learn about the major theories and approaches to teaching composition. I have found that utilizing maps, parodies, comics, trading cards, and other unusual genres enhances learning about a large body of complex information (see Mack, 2009). In particular, parody gives students a way to humorously characterize differences among academic theories by portraying a particular group's favorite type of beer, vacation destination, superhero, and so forth. When they shared their humorous portrayals in class, students gained confidence in using difficult concepts, terminology, and scholars' names. The mapping, parody, and poetry genres were pre-writing for an academic essay that students composed. In addition, students reported in their reflections that the inclusion of an unusual genre of their choice developed and supplemented their academic essay. For teachers who see multigenre as less than academic, the additional genres can be viewed as supports and extensions for a traditional essay or report. However, academic writing is becoming more and more multigenre and will continue to advance in its use of multimedia and multimodalities to deliver information.

Good writing never does just one thing. Good writing utilizes multiple strategies and skills to effectively communicate several goals, whether those goals are to reflect, describe, analyze, critique, and/or advocate a particular topic or content. When thoughtfully designed, multigenre projects offer writers the ability to demonstrate an abundance of the strategies, skills, and goals of good writing. A well-written, attractive multigenre project is worthy of being shared and celebrated—and is the best testimonial for the effectiveness of this pedagogy.

Correlations Between the Common Core State Standards and Minilessons and Activities

The Common Core College and Career Readiness Anchor Standards for grades 6–12 are listed in the center column, and the Minilessons and Activities from this book are listed in the right column.

Reading—Informational

	Anchor Standards	Minilessons and Activities
Key Ideas and Details	RI.1 Read closely to determine what the text says explicitly and to make logical inferences from it; cite specific textual evidence when writing or speaking to support conclusions drawn from the text.	Ch. 1 Strategies 1 Ch. 4 Motivators 3 Ch. 7 Motivators 2 Ch. 7 Strategies 2
	RI.2 Determine central ideas or themes of a text and analyze their development; summarize the key supporting details and ideas.	Ch. 2 Minilesson 2 Ch. 7 Motivators 1
	RI.3 Analyze how and why individuals, events, and ideas develop and interact over the course of a text.	Ch. 6 Tips 2 Ch. 7 Motivators 3

(continued)

	Anchor Standards	Minilessons and Activities
Craft and Structure	RI.4 Interpret words and phrases as they are used in a text, including determining technical, connotative, and figurative meanings, and analyze how specific word choices shape meaning or tone.	Ch. 4 Minilesson 3 Ch. 4 Tips 1 Ch. 7 Strategies 2
	RI.5 Analyze the structure of texts, including how specific sentences, paragraphs, and larger portions of the text (e.g., a section, chapter, scene, or stanza) relate to each other and the whole.	Ch. 2 Motivators 1 Ch. 3 Minilesson 1 Ch. 6 Motivators 1 & 2 Ch. 6 Minilesson 1 Ch. 6 Strategies 1
	RI.6 Assess how point of view or purpose shapes the content and style of a text.	Ch. 7 Strategies 2
Integration of Knowledge and Ideas	RI.7 Integrate and evaluate content presented in diverse formats and media, including visually and quantitatively, as well as in words.	Ch. 2 Strategies 2 Ch. 8 Motivators 1, 2, & 4 Ch. 8 Strategies 2
	RI.8 Delineate and evaluate the argument and specific claims in a text, including the validity of the reasoning as well as the relevance and sufficiency of the evidence.	Ch. 2 Tips 1 Ch. 7 Motivators 3
	RI.9 Analyze how two or more texts address similar themes or topics in order to build knowledge or to compare the approaches the authors take.	Ch. 3 Motivators 2 Ch. 4 Motivators 1 & 5 Ch. 6 Motivators 2 Ch. 6 Tips 2 Ch. 7 Strategies 2
Range of Reading and Level of Text Complexity	RI.10 Read and comprehend complex literary and informational texts independently and proficiently.	Accomplished during the whole project

Reading—Literature

	Anchor Standards	Minilessons and Activities
Key Ideas and Details	RL.1 Read closely to determine what the text says explicitly and to make logical inferences from it; cite specific textual evidence when writing or speaking to support conclusions drawn from the text.	Ch. 10 See literature projects in Linking Other Curricular Content Areas
	RL.2 Determine central ideas or themes of a text and analyze their development; summarize the key supporting details and ideas.	Ch. 10 See literature projects in Linking Curricular Content Areas
	RL.3 Analyze how and why individuals, events, and ideas develop and interact over the course of a text.	Ch. 4 Minilesson 1 Ch. 4 Strategies 2 Ch. 5 Minilesson 1 Ch. 10 See literature projects in Linking Curricular Content Areas
Craft and Structure	RL.4 Interpret words and phrases as they are used in a text, including determining technical, connotative, and figurative meanings, and analyze how specific word choices shape meaning or tone.	Ch. 5 Motivators 2 & 3 Ch. 5 Strategies 2
	RL.5 Analyze the structure of texts, including how specific sentences, paragraphs, and larger portions of the text (e.g., a section, chapter, scene, or stanza) relate to each other and the whole.	Ch. 4 Motivators 1 & 2 Ch. 5 Motivators 1
	RL.6 Assess how point of view or purpose shapes the content and style of a text.	Ch. 4 Motivators 1, 2, & 5 Ch. 4 Minilesson 1 Ch. 4 Strategies 1 Ch. 5 Strategies 1 Ch. 5 Motivators 4

(continued)

	Anchor Standards	Minilessons and Activities
Integration of Knowledge and Ideas	RL.7 Integrate and evaluate content presented in diverse formats and media, including visually and quantitatively, as well as in words.	Ch. 3 Motivators 3 Ch. 4 Motivators 2 Ch. 5 Tips 2
	RL.9 Analyze how two or more texts address similar themes or topics in order to build knowledge or to compare the approaches the authors take.	Ch. 4 Motivators 2 & 4 Ch. 5 Motivators 4
Range of Reading and Level of Text Complexity	RL.10 Read and comprehend complex literary and informational texts independently and proficiently.	Accomplished during the whole project

Writing

	Anchor Standards	Minilessons and Activities
Text Types and Purposes	W.1 Write arguments to support claims in an analysis of substantive topics or texts, using valid reasoning and relevant and sufficient evidence.	Ch. 7 All sections
	W.2 Write informative/explanatory texts to examine and convey complex ideas and information clearly and accurately through the effective selection, organization, and analysis of content.	Ch. 5 Motivators 1 Ch. 6 All sections
	W.3 Write narratives to develop real or imagined experiences or events using effective technique, well-chosen details, and well-structured event sequences.	Ch. 4 All sections

		Anchor Standards	Minilessons and Activities
Production and Distribution of Writing	W.4	Produce clear and coherent writing in which the development, organization, and style are appropriate to task, purpose, and audience.	Ch. 3 Strategies 1 & 2 Ch. 3 Tips 1 Ch. 4 Minilesson 3 The completed project
	W.5	Develop and strengthen writing as needed by planning, revising, editing, rewriting, or trying a new approach.	Ch. 1 Motivators 4 Ch. 1 Minilessons 1 & 2 Ch. 3 Strategies 1 & 2 Ch. 3 Tips 2, 3, & 4 Ch. 4 Motivators 4 & 5 Ch. 4 Minilessons 1, 2, & 3 Ch. 4 Tips 1 & 2 Ch. 5 Minilessons 1 & 2 Ch. 5 Strategies 1 & 2 Ch. 5 Tips 2 Ch. 6 Minilesson 2 Ch. 7 Minilessons 1 & 2 Ch. 7 Strategies 1 Ch. 7 Tips 1 Ch. 9 Minilessons 2 & 3 Ch. 9 Tips 1
	W.6	Use technology, including the Internet, to produce and publish writing and to interact and collaborate with others.	Ch. 5 Tips 2 Ch. 8 Minilesson 2

(continued)

	Anchor Standards	Minilessons and Activities
Research to Build and Present Knowledge	W.7 Conduct short as well as more sustained research projects based on focused questions, demonstrating understanding of the subject under investigation.	Ch. 2 Motivators 2 & 3 Ch. 3 Minilesson 1
	W.8 Gather relevant information from multiple print and digital sources, assess the credibility and accuracy of each source, and integrate the information while avoiding plagiarism.	Ch. 2 Minilesson 1 Ch. 2 Strategies 1 Ch. 2 Tips 1 & 2 Ch. 6 Minilesson 2
	W.9 Draw evidence from literary or informational texts to support analysis, reflection, and research.	Ch. 2 Minilesson 2 Ch. 7 Minilesson 2
Range of Writing	W.10 Write routinely over extended time frames (time for research, reflection, and revision) and shorter time frames (a single sitting or a day or two) for a range of tasks, purposes, and audiences.	Accomplished during the whole project

Speaking and Listening

	Anchor Standards	Minilessons and Activities
Comprehension and Collaboration	SL.1 Prepare for and participate effectively in a range of conversations and collaborations with diverse partners, building on others' ideas and expressing their own clearly and persuasively.	Introduction, Planning, and Organizing Ch. 1 Motivators 3 Ch. 1 Minilesson 1 Ch. 1 Strategies 2 Ch. 1 Tips 1 & 2 Ch. 2 Motivators 2 Ch. 2 Minilesson 2 Ch. 2 Tips 1 & 2 Ch. 3 Motivators 2, 3, & 4 Ch. 3 Minilesson 2 Ch. 4 Motivators 1 & 2 Ch. 4 Tips 1 Ch. 5 Motivators 2 & 3 Ch. 5 Strategies 1 Ch. 6 Motivators 2 Ch. 7 Motivators 1, 2, and 3 Ch. 7 Development Minilesson Ch. 7 Strategies 2 Ch. 8 Strategies 2 Ch. 8 Tips 1
	SL.2 Integrate and evaluate information presented in diverse media and formats, including visually, quantitatively, and orally.	Ch. 8 Strategies 2
	SL.3 Evaluate a speaker's point of view, reasoning, and use of evidence and rhetoric.	Ch. 7 Motivators 4

(continued)

	Anchor Standards	Minilessons and Activities
Presentation of Knowledge and Ideas	SL.4 Present information, findings, and supporting evidence such that listeners can follow the line of reasoning and the organization, development, and style are appropriate to task, purpose, and audience.	Ch. 3 Minilesson 2 Ch. 6 Motivators 2 Ch. 7 Minilesson 2 Ch. 9 Motivators 3 & 4
	SL.5 Make strategic use of digital media and visual displays of data to express information and enhance understanding of presentations.	Ch. 9 Tips 2 Ch. 8 Motivators 3 Ch. 8 Minilesson 1 Ch. 8 Strategies 1 & 2 Ch. 8 Tips 2
	SL.6 Adapt speech to a variety of contexts and communicative tasks, demonstrating command of formal English when indicated or appropriate.	Ch. 7 Minilesson 2 Ch. 9 Motivators 4

Language

		Anchor Standards	Minilessons and Activities
Conventions of Standard English	L.1	Demonstrate command of the conventions of standard English grammar and usage when writing or speaking.	Ch. 4 Motivators 5 Ch. 4 Tips 4 Ch. 5 Tips 1 Ch. 7 Tips 2 Ch. 9 Minilesson 3 Ch. 9 Strategies 1
	L.2	Demonstrate command of the conventions of standard English capitalization, punctuation, and spelling when writing.	Ch. 4 Tips 3 Ch. 6 Strategies 2 Ch. 6 Tips 1 Ch. 9 Minilesson 3 Ch. 9 Strategies 1
Knowledge of Language	L.3	Apply knowledge of language to understand how language functions in different contexts, to make effective choices for meaning or style, and to comprehend more fully when reading or listening.	Ch. 4 Tips 1 & 2 Ch. 6 Strategies 1 Ch. 7 Tips 1
Vocabulary Acquisition and Use	L.4	Determine or clarify the meaning of unknown and multiple-meaning words and phrases by using context clues, analyzing meaningful word parts, and consulting general and specialized reference materials, as appropriate.	Ch. 1 Motivators 2
	L.5	Demonstrate understanding of word relationships and nuances in word meanings.	Ch. 4 Motivators 2 Ch. 5 Strategies 2
	L.6	Acquire and use accurately a range of general academic and domain-specific words and phrases sufficient for reading, writing, speaking, and listening at the college and career readiness level; demonstrate independence in gathering vocabulary knowledge when considering a word or phrase important to comprehension or expression.	Ch. 1 Motivators 1 & 2 Ch. 3 Motivators 1 & 2 Ch. 7 Minilesson 2

References

Achebe, C. (1994). *Things fall apart*. New York, NY: Anchor Books.

Allen, C. A. (2001). *The multigenre research paper: Voice, passion, and discovery in grades 4–6*. Portsmouth, NH: Heinemann.

Anyon, J. (1981). Social class and the hidden curriculum of work. *Journal of Education, 162*(1), 67–92.

Bakhtin, M. M. (1981). *The dialogic imagination: Four essays*. Austin, TX: University of Texas Press.

Bawarshi, A., & Reiff, M. J. (2010). *Genre: An introduction to history, theory, research, and pedagogy*. Fort Collins, CO: WAC Clearinghouse and Parlor Press.

Beah, I. (2007). *A long way gone: Memoirs of a boy soldier*. New York, NY: Farrar, Straus and Giroux.

Britton, J. N., Burgess, T., Martin, N., McLeod, A., & Rosen, H. (1975). *The development of writing abilities (11–18)*. London, England: MacMillan Education.

Butler, P. (2002). Imitation as freedom: Reforming student writing. *The Quarterly: Journal of the National Writing Project, 24*(2), 25–32. Available at www.nwp.org/cs/public/print/resource/361

Connors, R. J. (1981). The rise and fall of the modes of discourse. *College Composition and Communication, 32*(4), 444–455.

Crawford, M. B. (2015). *The world beyond your head: On becoming an individual in the age of distraction*. New York, NY: Farrar, Straus, and Giroux.

Damasio, A. R. (1999). *The feeling of what happens: Body and emotion in the making of consciousness*. New York, NY: Harcourt Brace.

Davis, R. L., & Shadle, M. F. (2007). *Teaching multiwriting: Researching and composing with multiple genres, media, disciplines, and cultures*. Carbondale, IL: Southern Illinois University Press.

Devitt, A. J. (2014). "Genre pedagogies." In G. Tate, A. R. Taggart, K. Schick, & H. B. Hessler (Eds.), *A guide to composition pedagogies* (2nd ed.; pp. 146–162). New York, NY: Oxford University Press.

Diederich, P. (2006). In praise of praise. In Richard Straub (Ed.), *Key works on teacher response: An anthology* (pp. 221–224). Portsmouth, NH: Boynton/Cook.

Dixon, J. (1969). *Growth through English: A report based on the Dartmouth Seminar, 1966*. Reading, England: National Association for the Teaching of English.

Dragga, S. (1988). The effects of praiseworthy grading on students and teachers. *Journal of Teaching Writing, 7*(1), 41–50.

Dunbar, P. L., & Braxton, J. M. (1993). *The collected poetry of Paul Laurence Dunbar*. Charlottesville, VA: University Press of Virginia.

Fish, S. (2010, August 9). Plagiarism is not a big moral deal. *New York Times*. Available at opinionator.blogs.nytimes.com

Fleckenstein, K. S., Calendrillo, L. T., & Worley, D. A. (2002). *Language and image in the reading-writing classroom: Teaching vision*. Mahwah, NJ: Lawrence Erlbaum Associates.

Fleischman, P., & Beddows, E. (1988). *Joyful noise: Poems for two voices*. New York, NY: Harper & Row.

Friedmann, T. (1983). Teaching error, nurturing confusion: Grammar texts, tests, and teachers in the developmental English class. *College English, 45*(4), 390–399.

Gearhart, S. M. (1979). The womanization of rhetoric. *Women's Studies International Quarterly, 2*(2), 195–201.

Gendler, J. R. (1988). *The book of qualities*. New York, NY: Perennial.

Green, J. (2012). *The fault in our stars*. New York, NY: Dutton.

Harris, J. (1987). Proofreading: A reading/writing skill. *College Composition and Communication, 38*, 4, 464–466.

Haswell, R. H. (1983). Minimal marking. *College English, 45*(6), 600–604.

Heath, S. B. (1983). *Ways with words: Language, life, and work in communities and classrooms*. New York, NY: Cambridge University Press.

Herrick, J. A. (2005). *The history and theory of rhetoric: An introduction*. Boston, MA: Allyn & Bacon.

Hill, B. (2012, February 28). Inner dialogue—Writing character thoughts. The editor's blog. Available at http://theeditorsblog.net/2012/02/28/inner-dialogue-writing-character-thoughts/

Hosseini, K. (2007). *A thousand splendid suns*. New York, NY: Riverhead Books.

Huttenlocher, J., & Prohaska, V. (1997). Reconstructing the times of past events. In N. Stein. P. A. Ornstein, B. Tversky, & C. Brainerd (Eds.), *Memory for everyday events* (pp. 165–180). Mahwah, NJ: Lawrence Erlbaum Associates.

Hyland, K. (2002). Authority and invisibility: Authorial identity in academic writing. *Journal of Pragmatics, 34*(8), 1091–1112.

Hyland, K. (2004). *Disciplinary discourses: Social interactions in academic writing*. Ann Arbor, MI: University of Michigan Press.

Irvine, J., & Reid, B. (1987). *How to make pop-ups*. New York, NY: Morrow Junior Books.

Jocson, K. M. (2012). Youth media as narrative assemblage: examining new literacies at an urban high school. *Pedagogies: an International Journal, 7*(4), 298–316.

Johnson, C. L., & Moneysmith, J. (2005). *Multiple genres, multiple voices: Teaching argument in composition and literature*. Portsmouth, NH: Boynton/Cook.

Jung, J. (2005). *Revisionary rhetoric, feminist pedagogy, and multigenre texts*. Carbondale, IL: Southern Illinois University Press.

Kellogg, S. (1995). *Sally Ann Thunder Ann Whirlwind Crockett: A tall tale*. New York, NY: Morrow Junior Books.

Kimmel, H. (2001). *A girl named Zippy: Growing up small in Mooreland, Indiana*. New York, NY: Doubleday.

Klose, S. (1999). A graduation poem for two. *Center for Children and Technology*. Available at http://cct2.edc.org/NDL/1999/lessons/teams/17/poem2.html

Kuh, G. D., Kinzie, J., Schuh, J. H., & Whitt, E. J. (2010). *Student success in college: Creating conditions that matter.* San Francisco, CA: John Wiley & Sons.

Langer, J. A., & Flihan, S. (2000). Writing and reading relationships: Constructive tasks. In R. Indrisano & J. Squire (Eds.), *Perspectives on the writing process: Research, theory, and practice.* Newark, DE: International Reading Association. Available at www.albany.edu/cela/publication/article/writeread.htm

Larson, R. L. (1982). The "research paper" in the writing course: A non-form of writing. *College English, 44*(8), 811–816.

Lyon, G. E. (1999). *Where I'm from: Where poems come from.* Spring, TX: Absey & Co.

Mack, N. (2002). The ins, outs, and in-betweens of multigenre writing. *English Journal, 92*(2), 91–98.

Mack, N. (2005). *Teaching grammar with playful poems.* New York, NY: Scholastic.

Mack, N. (2006). Ethical representation of working-class lives: Multiple genres, voices, and identities. *Pedagogy, 6*(1), 53–78.

Mack, N. (2008). *Teaching grammar with perfect poems for middle school.* New York, NY: Scholastic.

Mack, N. (2009). Representations of the field in graduate courses: Using parody to question all positions. *College English, 71*(5), 435–459.

Mack, N. (2013). Colorful revision: Color-coded comments connected to instruction. *Teaching English in the Two-Year College, 40*(3), 248–256.

Mack, N. (2014). Critical memoir and identity formation: Being, belonging, becoming. In R. Gatto & T. Roeder (Eds.), *Critical expressivist practices in the college writing classroom* (pp. 55–68). Anderson, SC: Parlor Press.

McCloud, S. (1994). *Understanding comics.* New York, NY: Perennial.

McCloud, S. (2000). *Reinventing comics.* New York, NY: Perennial.

McCloud, S. (2006). *Making comics: Storytelling secrets of comics, manga and graphic novels.* New York, NY: Perennial.

Melville, H. (1990). *Billy Budd.* Raleigh, NC: Alex Catalogue.

Moffett, J. (1965). I, you, and it. *College Composition and Communication, 16*(5), 243–248.

Moffett, J. (1973). *Interaction: A student centered language arts and reading program.* Boston, MA: Houghton Mifflin.

Moll, L. C. (2014). *L.S. Vygotsky and education.* New York, NY: Routledge.

Montgomery, M.-M. (2009). *First-year students' perception and interpretation of teacher response to their writing: Ten students speak.* Amherst, MA: University of Massachusetts Amherst.

Munsch, R. N., & Martchenko, M. (2006). *The paperbag princess.* Lindfield, New South Wales: Scholastic Australia.

Murray, D. M. (1998). *The craft of revision.* Fort Worth, TX: Harcourt Brace.

Murray, J. (2009). *Non-discursive rhetoric: Image and affect in multimodal composition.* Albany, NY: SUNY Press.

Myers, W. D., & Myers, C. (1999). *Monster.* New York, NY: HarperCollins.

National Council of Teachers of English position statement. (1974). Resolution on students' right to their own language. Available at www.ncte.org/positions/statements/righttoownlanguage

O'Brien, T. (1998). *The things they carried: A work of fiction.* New York, NY: Broadway Books.

Ogbu, J. U., & Simons, H. D. (1998). Voluntary and involuntary minorities: A cultural-ecological theory of school performance with some implications for education. *Anthropology & Education Quarterly. 29*(2), 155–188.

Paul, A. M. (2012, March 17). Your brain on fiction. *New York Times Magazine.* Available at www.nytimes.com/2012/03/18/opinion/sunday/the-neuroscience-of-your-brain-on-fiction.html?pagewanted=all&_r=0

Picoult, J. (2004). *My sister's keeper: A novel.* New York, NY: Atria Books.

Pinker, S. (1997). *How the mind works.* New York, NY: Norton.

Preston, J. (2015). (Project)ing literacy: Writing to assemble in a postcomposition fyw classroom. *College, Composition, and Communication,* forthcoming.

Ramachandran, V. S., & Blakeslee, S. (1998). *Phantoms in the brain: Probing the mysteries of the human mind.* New York, NY: William Morrow.

Rogers, C. R., & Roethlisberger, F. J. (1952). *Barriers and gateways to communication.* Boston, MA: Harvard Business Review Reprint Service.

Rohan, L. (2004). I remember mamma: Material rhetoric, mnemonic activity, and one woman's turn-of-the-twentieth-century quilt. *Rhetoric Review, 23*(4), 368–387.

Romano, T. (1988, October). The multigenre research paper. Third Miami University Conference on the Teaching of Writing: The Writing Teacher as Researcher, Oxford, OH.

Romano, T. (1995). *Writing with passion: Life stories, multiple genres.* Portsmouth, NH: Boynton/Cook.

Romano, T. (2000). *Blending genre, altering style: Writing multigenre papers.* Portsmouth, NH: Boynton/Cook.

Romano, T. (2013). *Fearless writing: Multigenre to motivate and inspire.* Portsmouth, NH: Heinemann

Seitz, D. (2014). Place-based genre writing as critical expressivist practice. In R. Gatto & T. Roeder (Eds.), *Critical expressivist practices in the college writing classroom* (pp. 249–260). Anderson, SC: Parlor Press.

Seuss, Dr., Prelutsky, J., & Smith, L. (1998). *Hooray for Diffendoofer Day!* New York, NY: Knopf.

Simons, E. R. (1990). *Student worlds, student words: Teaching writing through folklore.* Portsmouth, NH: Boynton/Cook.

Thoreau, H. D. (1971) In J. L. Shanley (Ed.), *Walden.* Princeton, NJ: Princeton University Press.

Toulmin, S. E. (2003). *The uses of argument.* Cambridge, England: Cambridge University Press.

Vare, R., & Smith, D. B. (Eds.). (2007). *The American idea: The best of the Atlantic monthly: 150 years of writers and thinkers who shaped our history.* New York, NY: Doubleday.

Viorst, J., & Cherry, L. (1981). *If I were in charge of the world and other worries: Poems for children and their parents.* New York, NY: Atheneum.

Vygotsky, L. S. (1978). *Mind in society: The development of higher psychological processes.* Cambridge, MA: Harvard University Press.

Walls, J. (2005). *The glass castle: A memoir.* New York, NY: Scribner.

Weaver, C. (2002). *Reading process and practice.* Portsmouth, NH: Heinemann.

Weber-Wulff, D. (2014). *False feathers: A perspective on academic plagiarism.* Berlin, Germany: Springer.

Wheeler, L. K. (n.d.). Style comparisons: Different authors? Available at https://web.cn.edu/kwheeler/style2.html

Wiesel, E., & Wiesel, M. (2006). *Night*. New York, NY: Hill and Wang, a division of Farrar, Straus and Giroux.

Yankovic, Al. (2014, July 15). Word crimes. Available at www.youtube.com/watch?v=8Gv0H-vPoDc

Youngs, S., & Barone, D. M. (2007). *Writing without boundaries: What's possible when students combine genres*. Portsmouth, NH: Heinemann.

Zeitlin, S. J., Kotkin, A., Baker, H. C., & Festival of American Folklife. (1982). *A celebration of American family folklore: Tales and traditions from the Smithsonian collection*. New York, NY: Pantheon Books.

Index

About the Author

Dr. Nancy Mack is a professor of English at Wright State University, where she teaches both undergraduate and graduate courses in writing. Her publications include books about teaching grammar with poetry, chapters in books, and articles in numerous academic journals. She has participated in several grants, including the National Endowment for the Arts and PBS multimedia programs for teachers. Nancy Mack's career started as a middle and high school teacher, and she has taught in three prison programs. She is a frequent speaker at national and state conferences as well as district inservices, and she has won several teaching awards.